The principal objective of THE MATHESON TRUST is to promote the study of comparative religion from the point of view of the underlying harmony of the great religious and philosophical traditions of the world. This objective is being pursued through such means as audio-visual media, the support and sponsorship of lecture series and conferences, the creation of a website, collaboration with film production companies and publishing companies as well as the Trust's own series of publications.

The Matheson Monographs cover a wide range of themes within the field of comparative religion: scriptural exegesis in different religious traditions; the modalities of spiritual and contemplative life; in-depth mystical studies of particular religious traditions; broad comparative analyses taking in a series of religious forms; studies of traditional arts, crafts and cosmological science; and contemporary scholarly expositions of religious philosophy and metaphysics. The monographs also comprise translations of both classical and contemporary texts, as well as transcriptions of lectures by, and interviews with, spiritual and scholarly authorities from different religious and philosophical traditions.

WEIGHING THE WORD

•

REASONING THE QUR'ĀN AS REVELATION

إِنَّا سَنُلْقِى عَلَيْكَ قَوْلًا ثَقِيلًا

Behold, We shall cast upon thee a weighty word

QUR'ĀN 73:5

WEIGHING THE WORD

Reasoning the Qur'ān
as
Revelation

by

Peter Samsel

THE MATHESON TRUST
For the Study of Comparative Religion

This first edition published by
The Matheson Trust
PO Box 336
56 Gloucester Road
London SW7 4UB, UK

www.themathesontrust.org

ISBN: 978 1 908092 14 4

Typeset by the publishers in Baskerville 10 Pro

Cover: Iskandar (Alexander) with the seven sages.
Detail from a 15th c. manuscript of Nizami's *Khamsah*.
© The British Library Board, Or. 6810, f.214.

Arabic calligraphies by Hasan Kan'an (Arts College),
courtesy of www.FREEISLAMICCALLIGRAPHY.com,
© The Prince Ghazi Trust for Qur'anic Thought.

Contents

For James Cutsinger

Introduction

The most important and indeed most obvious question that may be asked regarding the Qur'ān is that addressing its ostensibly revelatory character. Simply put, is it the word of God, as it claims to be, or not? For the Islamic community, taken in the fullness of its course and span, the answer has seemed perfectly, indeed blindingly, self-evident. For those in the West, whether past or present, whether Christian or secular modern, the answer has, until quite recently, also seemed perfectly self-evident. These answers have, needless to say, been not merely distinct but oppositional. None of this is particularly surprising. Quite generally, the matter of the acceptance or rejection of a claimed revelation frequently and naturally polarizes between those within a given faith community who naturally and dispositionally accept the ostensible revelation and those outside of it, particularly those of a rival "faith community"—whether religious or secular—who in their turn naturally and dispositionally reject the claimed revelation. Historical experience teaches that those inside and outside of such a faith community are rarely unpersuaded from their respectively normative views just as they are rarely persuasive to one another's. All of these observations are particularly true with respect to the normative judgments regarding the Qur'ān to be found in Islam and the West. In one respect, relatively little has shifted in outlook in the nearly thirteen centuries since the earliest Christian polemic against Islam. As Richard Fletcher has sagely observed in this regard, "Attitudes laid down like rocks long ago continue to shape their moral environment for many centuries thereafter. There is a geology of human relationships which it is unwise to neglect."[1]

Nevertheless, while the rise of secular modernity has certainly complicated the orientation of the West with regard to the question of the Qur'ān,[2] there has also been, more recently, a reevaluation, if not quite a rapprochement, within Christianity itself. In this latter regard, three touchstones of particular note may be mentioned: First, the pontifical declaration *Nostra Aetate* (*On the Relation of the Church to Non-Christian Religions*)[3] of Pope Paul VI; second, the many positive statements and interactions of Pope John Paul II with respect to Islam and Muslims over the course of his pontificate;[4] third and most recently, the *Common Word* initiative, launched initially as an open letter signed by a large, representative body of Muslim scholars and religious authorities addressing Christian leaders worldwide, which has grown to become the most significant and successful platform for Muslim-Christian interreligious dialogue in history.[5]

In any weighing of judgment with regard to a claimed revelation such as the Qur'ān, it is never the case that disinterested reasoned argument is the sole consideration; rather, factors related to identity, will and sentiment also contribute. Sound arguments may be given, but none will be persuasive to all individuals. For a faith community, the putting forth of such arguments is nevertheless a necessary exercise, and perhaps for three reasons: a) to comfort the faithful; b) to possibly persuade those neutral; and c) to not unnecessarily cede argumentative ground to those in opposition. The impartial consideration of such arguments may well also be considered a necessary exercise for those opposed, if for nothing else as a potential corrective to possible misunderstandings or misjudgments. This aside, however, one may also simply try to approach the question as dispassionately as possible—however imperfectly this may be achieved—and in view of what considerations may be brought to bear, evaluate what judgment, however personal and tentative, may be made.

The present monograph, which is aligned most closely with this final, dispassionate mode of engagement, is an exercise in what might be termed "exploratory apologetics". It is an attempt, no doubt particular and incomplete, to discover, sort through and posit what considerations and arguments may be brought to bear in respect of the Qur'ān's revelatory status. Many of the considerations presented are well known—at least by those who take an interest in such matters—while some are quite recent, even cutting-edge, and a few are, to our knowledge, original, either in conception or application, to the question at hand. Our aim in this is at once comprehensive and modest: we have not included every possible argument— some will no doubt have escaped our attention; others we have considered weak or problematic; still others are of note and value, but of a detailed technical nature beyond the scope of a presentation such as this. Further, we have, in the interest of space, merely surveyed many of the considerations presented, quoting liberally from relevant sources and noting additional resources for the reader where applicable. For a certain type of Muslim reader, challenged in faith by the worldview of secular modernity, the considerations presented may well be found to serve as a help and support. For a non-Muslim reader—whether secular, Christian, Jew or other—these same considerations may well demonstrate that the question of the Qur'ān's revelatory status is, at the very least, to be regarded as a serious one.

At this point, a mild suggestion may be in order. Ideally, the present monograph should never have been written nor needed to have been written, as the material it covers should have been addressed well before and by more able individuals. By way of contrast, Western Christianity—both Catholic and Protestant—has a developed apologetical tradition for the rational defense of its faith. This is, with a handful of noteworthy exceptions,[6] largely not the case with contemporary Islam. As Shabbir Akhtar has observed:

> Unlike their Christian rivals, Muslims have not produced a philosophical defense of the rationality of Islamic theism in the modern world. Christianity has developed continuous and distinguished philosophical and apologetic traditions; Christians have always responded to the rational pressures of secularism in order to reconcile traditional faith with hostile skeptical secularism.[7]

In part, this distinction is due to particular circumstances within each faith: Western Christianity has known the doctrinal and existential threat of secular modernity longer and more intimately than any other tradition—having nurtured its mortal enemy in its own bosom—and has been forced to respond accordingly. Islam, comparatively sheltered from this same threat for a longer period, has ever had the example of the Qur'ān before it, which has been quite capable, even at this late hour, of arguing for itself without the need of human apologetical intervention. Nevertheless, the historical situation has altered for Muslims, and apologetics has perhaps become necessary in a way that was largely not historically required by the Islamic community. However, from what we have seen, it would appear that most would-be Muslim apologists are hardly even aware of Christian apologetical sources, from which they could learn much. Certainly, the bulk of Christian philosophical apologetics—most notably in the context of classical theism—may be taken up whole cloth and applied, often with better justification, in defense of specifically Qur'ānic teachings. Such application is particularly pertinent with respect to specifically secular challenges to faith typical of the contemporary situation. The attentive reader will note that the first section of the monograph is an exercise in just this type of engagement.

Our foremost concern in the present work has not been for

the Qur'ān *per se* so much as for the Qur'ān as a particular instance and evidence of the reality of the transcendent. Muslim readers may quite obviously have an interest in the considerations we present upon the Qur'ān in the specific context of their Islamic faith. We would also suggest that, in the contemporary context, readers of other faith traditions may also have a vested, if possibly conflicted, interest in the Qur'ān as conceivably revelatory. The Qur'ān has, at the very least, the appearance of a major irruption of the transcendent into the human domain. Any such irruption—whether the revelation on Mt. Sinai, the birth of Christ, the descent of the Holy Spirit at Pentecost, or others further afield—is, we would argue, sufficiently rare and precious as to be of intrinsic interest, even if falling outside of the fold of one's own faith. Particularly in an era when religious traditions are challenged in their very root convictions as perhaps never before, a significant indication of the presence and action of the transcendent, even from another tradition, may serve indirectly as a bulwark of one's own faith, even as a consolation. In this regard, the words of Pope Pius XII have a certain pertinence: "How consoling it is for me to know that, all over the world, millions of people, five times a day, bow down before God."[8]

Peter Samsel

Notes to Introduction

1. Richard Fletcher, *The Cross and the Crescent: Christianity and Islam from Muhammad to the Reformation* (London: Penguin, 2004), p. 159.
2. Sometimes in surprising ways: see, for instance, Ziad Elmarsafy, *The Enlightenment Qur'ān: The Politics of Translation and the Construction of Islam* (Oxford, UK: Oneworld, 2009).
3. http://tinyurl.com/vati-nostra. [PUBLISHER'S NOTE: All referenced URLs have been verified upon the date of publication.]
4. http://tinyurl.com/usccb-muslims.
5. www.acommonword.com.
6. See, for instance, Shabbir Akhtar, *The Qur'ān and the Secular Mind: A Philosophy of Islam* (London: Routledge, 2008); also Muḥammad Muṣṭafā al-Aʿẓamī, *The History of the Qur'ānic Text, from Revelation to Compilation: A Comparative Study with the Old and New Testaments* (Leicester, UK: UK Islamic Academy, 2003); also www.islamic-awareness.org.
7. Shabbir Akhtar, *The Qur'ān and the Secular Mind*, pp. 337–8.
8. William Stoddart, *What Do the Religions Say about Each Other?* (San Rafael, CA: Sophia Perennis, 2008), p. 12.

1

The Qur'ān and Secularity

1 · A The Problem of the Modern

1. A. 1 A Precommitment to Immanent Closure

In considering the status of the Qur'ān from within the context of secular modernity, one of the first requirements is to examine the often implicit assumptions of that context that in turn inform such a consideration. As Arthur O. Lovejoy has more generally observed:

> There are, first, implicit or incompletely explicit *assumptions*,
> or more or less *unconscious mental habits*, operating in the
> thought of an individual or a generation. It is the beliefs
> which are so much a matter of course that they are rather
> tacitly presupposed than formally expressed and argued for,
> the ways of thinking which seem so natural and inevitable
> that they are not scrutinized with the eye of logical self-
> consciousness, that often are most decisive of the character
> of a philosopher's doctrine, and still oftener of the dominant
> intellectual tendencies of an age.[1]

To be a modern, as opposed to simply inhabiting modernity, is, first and foremost, to accept, whether reflectively or
reflexively, the worldview of modernism, a worldview characterized most significantly by the rejection of the transcendent.
Charles Taylor, who has termed such a worldview the "closed
immanent frame", has traced in considerable detail the histori-

cal process of secularization that has led to a state such that "it [was] virtually impossible not to believe in God in, say, 1500 in our Western society, while in 2000 many of us find this not only easy, but even inescapable."[2] The acceptance of immanent closure, such that it appears obvious, natural or given, is based not so much upon careful argumentation as upon a general narrative or set of narratives. As Taylor has noted:

> The narrative dimension is extremely important, because the force of [the immanent frame] comes less from the supposed detail of the argument (that science refutes religion, or that Christianity is incompatible with human rights), and much more from the general form of the narratives, to the effect that there was once a time when religion could flourish, but that this time is past. The plausibility structures of faith have collapsed, once and for all, irreversibly.... And the same kind of supposition is widespread today, now in favor of atheism, or materialism, relegating all forms of religion to an earlier era. In a certain sense, the original arguments on which this narrative rests cease to matter, so powerful is the sense created in certain milieux, that these old views just *can't* be options for us.[3]

Commenting specifically on the dominance of a particularly constrictive or closed sense of the immanent frame within Western academia, he has further noted:

> In general, we have here what Wittgenstein calls a "picture", a background to our thinking, within whose terms it is carried on, but which is often largely unformulated, and to which we can frequently, just for this reason, imagine no alternative. As he once famously put it, "a picture held us captive."... Our predicament in the modern West is, therefore, not only characterized by what I have called the immanent frame, which we all more or less share... It also consists of more specific pictures, the immanent frame as "spun" in ways of openness and closure, which are often dominant in certain milieux. This local dominance obviously strengthens their

hold as pictures. The spin of closure which is hegemonic in the Academy is a case in point.[4]

Edward Feser, in reviewing the philosophic objections to scientism, has noted similarly:

> Now if scientism faces such grave difficulties, why are so many intelligent people drawn to it? The answer—to paraphrase a remark made by Wittgenstein in another context—is that "a picture holds them captive." Hypnotized by the unparalleled predictive and technological successes of modern science, they infer that scientism must be true, and that anything that follows from scientism—however fantastic or even seemingly incoherent—must also be true.[5]

For modern historians of religion, already in many instances doubly committed on a personal level to immanent closure, first as moderns and then again as academicians, there is yet another formal and methodological commitment to immanent closure in their work as historians. An early articulation of such a stance is that of Ernst Troeltsch, who asserted that modern historians should take a "purely scientific attitude to historical fact",[6] and who, in the third of his three principles of critical history, asserted that "The sole task of history in its specifically theoretical aspect is to explain every movement, process, state, and nexus of things by reference to the web of its causal relations."[7] A more recent asseveration of such a methodological commitment may be found in the work of Van Harvey. Although far more often assumed than stated or defended explicitly, such a "critical historical" approach takes as given that the admittance of the transcendent is out of bounds in any proper historical description.[8]

Western scholarship on the Qur'ān has been very much in line with this general attitude, as William A. Graham has noted:

> ... non-Muslim Qur'ān study has tended towards acceptance of, or acquiescence in, an Enlightenment naturalism or

3

materialism with respect to what it recognizes as "real." It has, in the main, isolated the intellectual and rational from the poetic and the religious and worked on the assumption that the former deal with what is "really real", by which is meant the phenomenal world of sense data. This excludes *a priori* the possibility of a numinous or transcendent dimension as a "given" in the "real" world.[9]

For most secular historians, such a precommitment seems not only natural but wholly justified, any alternative to which would take one at once outside of the domains of objectivity and rationality. There are, unfortunately, a number of problems implicit in such a stance, to be explored further below.

1. A. 2 Reason and the Incoherence of Immanent Closure

The most foundational issue regarding immanent closure, one that is at once obvious and yet strangely unnoticed, is its fundamental incoherence. Less severely, one may note its fundamental incompleteness, particularly with regard to the following broadly intractable issues: a) the bare fact of existence, particularly in light of temporal creation as indicated in astrophysical cosmology; b) the precise and elegant ordering of existence, both in terms of the physical laws as well as the values of the physical constants; c) the origin of life, which is a prior to any evolutionary explanation; d) the origin and nature of consciousness, which escapes a strict physicalism altogether; e) the coordination between the deep structure of natural order and the abstract ordering of our minds, as is singularly evident in such domains as mathematical physics.

Its incompleteness aside, its incoherence may be traced along a number of lines, including accounting under a strict physicalism, most typically taken as entailed under immanent closure, for such fundamental requirements as consciousness, subjectivity, unified personhood, free will, intentionality, reason, morality, meaning and value.[10] Such requirements are necessary for the articulation of any worldview, including that of immanent closure. As John Searle has noted:

> There is exactly one overriding question in contemporary philosophy... How do we fit in?... How can we square this self-conception of ourselves as mindful, meaning-creating, free, rational, etc., agents with a universe that consists entirely of mindless, meaningless, unfree, nonrational, brute physical particles?[11]

With regard to consciousness, necessarily entailed in all of the other requirements above, certain philosophers of mind have noted the profound disjunction between physical objects and states and the immediate experience of consciousness and mentation:

1) There is a raw qualitative feel or a "what it is like" to have a mental state such as a pain.

2) At least many mental states have intentionality—*ofness* or *aboutness*—directed towards an object.

3) Mental states are inner, private and immediate to the subject having them.

4) Mental states require a subjective ontology—namely, mental states are necessarily owned by the first person sentient subjects who have them.

5) Mental states fail to have crucial features (e.g., spatial extension, location) that characterize physical states and, in general, cannot be described using physical language.[12]

Such a disjunction becomes even more pronounced upon consideration of reason, in whose name the worldview of immanent closure so typically takes its stand. Ironically, it is precisely the general unaccountability of reason under immanent closure that provides one of the clearest indications of the fundamental incoherence of this worldview. As a broad summary of the issue, J. P. Moreland, in review of a recent work of Thomas Nagel, has commented:

> But there are several problems Nagel mentions with the naturalist attempt to account for the faculty of reason itself:
>
> 1) Reason isn't just pragmatically useful; indeed, it is self-refuting and circular to assert that it is.
>
> 2) Reason isn't a contingent, local, perspectivalist feature of our evolved nature. It has universal applicability. Evolution produces local, contingent dispositions, not universal, necessary ones.
>
> 3) Reason is intrinsically normative.
>
> 4) Reason takes us beyond appearances to the hidden, intelligible structure of the world.
>
> 5) In contrast to the senses, which put us in contact with objects via causal chains, reason is not mediated by mechanisms that could be selected by evolutionary processes; rather, reason puts us in immediate, direct contact with the rational order.
>
> 6) Reason is active and involves agency (for example, it isn't Sphexish [deterministic or preprogrammed]); sensation is passive.[13]

Each one of these considerations works to undermine any reduction of reason to a strictly naturalist conception consistent with the closed immanent frame. Taken in concert, they strongly indicate the radical insufficiency of any such project. To the contrary, reason bears every appearance of being, as it were, a "supernaturally natural" function within man that is, in itself, one of the clearest evidences tying man inextricably to the transcendent.

This incoherence of reason on a naturalist conception may be philosophically formalized, three examples of which are Victor Reppert and Alvin Plantinga's epistemic argument from reason,[14] Angus Menuge and J. P. Moreland's ontological argument from reason,[15] and James Ross and Edward Feser's argument for the necessary immateriality of reason.[16] The general lesson that may be drawn from all of these arguments is that the statement and defense of the naturalist worldview of immanent closure is articulated on the basis of human rationality, but this same rationality cannot be grounded within that worldview, thus undermining its very foundations.

1. A. 3 Meaning and the Incoherence of Immanent Closure

If immanent closure may be judged incoherent under a consideration of rationality, it may be similarly judged so under a consideration of meaning, intention, purpose and value. This is hardly a position that need even be philosophically argued for—it is, or should be, self-evident that a world reduced to "atoms and the void" is one necessarily revealed as nihilistic at its very core. As James W. Sire has noted:

> The strands of epistemological, metaphysical and ethical nihilism weave together to make a rope long enough and strong enough to hang a whole culture. The name of the rope is Loss of Meaning. We end in a total despair of ever seeing ourselves, the world and others as in any way significant. Nothing has meaning.... We have been thrown up by an impersonal universe. The moment a self-conscious, self-determining being appears on the scene, that person asks the big question: What is the meaning of all this? What is the purpose of the cosmos? But the person's creator— the impersonal forces of bedrock matter—cannot respond. If the cosmos is to have meaning, we must manufacture it for ourselves.... Thus does naturalism lead to nihilism. If we take seriously the implications of the death of God, the disappearance of the transcendent, the closedness of the universe, we end right there. Why, then, aren't most naturalists nihilists? The obvious answer is the best one: Most naturalists do not take their naturalism seriously. They are

inconsistent. They affirm a set of values. They have friends who affirm a similar set. They appear to know and don't ask how they know they know. They seem to be able to choose and don't ask themselves whether their apparent freedom is really caprice or determinism. Socrates said that the unexamined life is not worth living, but for a naturalist he is wrong. For a naturalist it is the examined life that is not worth living.[17]

As human beings, we cannot live the supposed "truth" of this condition, which would be as intolerable as the coldest depths of space. The modern, who accepts this "truth" but cannot live it, instead typically lives in a state of self-contradiction or self-deception regarding the catastrophic implications of his worldview, often living off of the husks of meaning and value inherent in a prior worldview now formally rejected. As John F. Haught has forcefully reminded:

> If the universe is meaningless, and ethics groundless, then truthfulness demands that one pass through the fires of nihilism before finding a post-religious comfort zone. But sunny naturalists have not yet looked down into the bottom of the abyss they have opened up. Instead they have nestled into the cultural and ethical worlds nurtured for centuries by worshipers of God. Surely naturalism has to have more disturbing implications than sunny naturalists are willing to entertain. If science has in truth dissolved the transcendent ground that formerly upheld nature and morality, then the sober naturalist wins the contest of candor hands down by at least trying to field the full implications of an essentially lifeless world.[18]

And further:

> ... the most rugged version of godlessness demands complete consistency. Go all the way and think the business of atheism through to the bitter end. This means that before you get too comfortable with the godless world you long for, you will be required by the logic of any consistent skepticism

to pass through the disorienting wilderness of nihilism. Do you have the courage to do that? You will have to adopt the tragic heroism of a Sisyphus, or realize that true freedom in the absence of God means that you are the creator of the values you live by. Don't you realize that this will be an intolerable burden from which most people will seek an escape? Are you ready to allow simple logic to lead you to the real truth about the death of God? Before settling into a truly atheistic worldview you will have to experience the Nietzschean madman's sensation of straying through "infinite nothingness." You will be required to summon up an unprecedented degree of courage if you plan to wipe away the whole horizon of transcendence. Are you willing to risk madness? If not, then you are not really an atheist.[19]

Under immanent closure, moderns may only live "as if" there were meaning, but to accept such an oblique, incoherent sense of meaning—no matter its ultimate illegitimacy—is necessary if they are to live at all. As Roger Scruton has wryly observed:

> To understand the depth of the... "as if" is to understand the condition of the modern soul. We know that we are animals, parts of the natural order, bound by laws which tie us to the material forces which govern everything. We believe that the gods are our invention, and that death is exactly what it seems. Our world has been disenchanted and our illusions destroyed. At the same time we cannot live as though that were the whole truth of our condition. Even modern people are compelled to praise and blame, love and hate, reward and punish. Even modern people—especially modern people—are aware of self, as the centre of their being; and even modern people try to connect to other selves around them. We therefore see others as if they were free beings, animated by a self or soul, and with more than a worldly destiny. If we abandon that perception, then human relations dwindle into a machine-like parody of themselves, the world is voided of love, duty and desire, and only the body remains... Modern science has presented us

with the "as ifness" of human freedom; but it could never equip us to live without the belief in it.[20]

Graham Dunstan Martin has similarly commented:

> Naturalism lays waste the world. It robs us of everything without exception. It denies that we perform even our own actions, and claims they are preordained by the purposeless accidents of blind causality, by the chatting up and down of mindless subatomic particles.... Yet we continue to desire to act, to desire to have powers, to believe in good and bad. It is as if we were normal active human beings till, just yesterday, the reductionist cast upon us the malevolent spell of his philosophy. Suddenly, if we believe him, we are paralyzed, helpless to act, victims of his metaphysics, immobilized and helpless like a paraplegic in a wheelchair. Along with our ability to move even a finger, he has filched away also our moral sense, our responsibility, all possibility of a meaning to our lives or even a sense to our words. The reductionist's world is not mere absence of sense, it is a kind of anti-meaning, a kind of despairing nihilism. It is as if there is, in his materialist universe, only one purpose left, namely to mock and decry all purposes.[21]

That moderns, living under immanent closure, should nonetheless be so resistant to recognizing the consequences of this closure—which resembles nothing so much as a collective failure of imagination—is at once a clear sign of its falsity while at the same time a barrier to its overturning. Nevertheless, such an insight may certainly be attained, in light of which the claims of modernity are revealed as a kind of hollow show. If neither reason nor value can be legitimately laid claim to, then neither can anything dependent upon these priors— a domain encompassing nearly all that is vital to human culture and flourishing. The shibboleths of the age, such as democracy and human rights, prove no exception, but are revealed as ungrounded as the rest. By what reason or value

10

may democracy, say, be asserted if both reason and value are fatally undermined?

A point that should perhaps be noted is that the appearance of purpose, meaning and value that we broadly and intrinsically seem to have is often taken by moderns as indicative of actual purpose, meaning and value, even in the face of the unavoidable nihilistic implications of immanent closure. The basic, if widespread, confusion is to assume that the mere fact of this appearance is sufficient to maintain the worldview of immanent closure and yet escape the nihilistic abyss. Upon reflection, however, it should be clear that exactly the opposite conclusion is indicated: the appearance of purpose, meaning and value is present precisely because there *is* actual purpose, meaning and value, but this actuality is grounded not in immanent closure, which is intrinsically incapable of sustaining it, but in a reality open to the transcendent domain, wherein it finds its necessary support.

One may broadly consider three possible stances with regard to the status of the closed immanent frame. The first, broadly accepted by most moderns, historians among them, is the normativity of immanent closure and the questionability of transcendence. The second, more generous stance—similar to what Stephen Jay Gould has termed "non-overlapping magisteria"[22]—might accept immanent closure and transcendence as distinct domains, if possibly rival "systems of faith". The third, which may even now be taken as the dominant view of humanity, is the questionability of immanent closure and the normativity of transcendence.

The evidence and arguments touched upon above strongly suggest that it is this third stance that must be taken as correct and that, in consequence, the closed immanent frame stands as a false foreclosure of the reality of transcendence.

1. A. 4 Three Traces of Transcendence

Three additional domains of human experience that may be brought to bear in challenge of immanent closure are: a) cross-cultural historical and contemporary accounts of miracles; b) cross-cultural historical and contemporary accounts of mystical experience; and c) philosophical proofs or arguments for the existence of the God of classical theism. All three of these domains have a direct bearing on the question of the revelatory status of the Qur'ān, which may be understood in terms of the Islamic tradition as at once a miraculous irruption in the world as well as a mystical unveiling of the divine Word. Further, insofar as God's existence may be strongly inferred on philosophical grounds, His revelation to man becomes far more likely, if indeed not to some extent anticipated.

With respect to miracles, the common wisdom is that the uniformity of scientific experience renders these impossible in principle. Under the assumption of immanent closure, this is a perfectly correct view. However, it is this very assumption that is presently open to question. Against such a view it may be noted that miraculous accounts are to be found both across civilizations as well as throughout history. In this respect, their sheer frequency, despite their inherent uncommonness, speaks against any dismissive evaluation. A particularly thorough resource for accounts of miracles across cultures is Kenneth L. Woodward's *The Book of Miracles*.[23] Taken in itself, such a study is open to the charge of a lack of suitably verifiable evidence associated with miraculous accounts. Another particularly thorough resource, one particularly germane to this issue, is Craig S. Keener's two-volume work *Miracles*.[24] Keener, although open to miraculous accounts from other religious traditions, is predominantly concerned with tracing and evaluating miracles in the context of Christianity from antiquity to the present day. A particular strength of Keener's work is the careful documentation of numerous contemporary case studies of miracles. Such documentation renders dismissal problematic, which problematizes in turn any blanket assumption regarding the impossibility of such accounts. Keener's work is also valuable for presenting much of the philosophical critique of David Hume's dismissal of miracles, one of the most notable points being its fundamental circularity: "Thus, on the usual reading of Hume, he manages to define away any possibility of a miracle occurring, by defining 'miracle' as a violation of natural law, yet defining 'natural law' as principles that cannot be violated."[25] In a specifically Islamic context, karāmāt (miracles) are frequently associated with saints or "friends of God". One resource that treats these in some detail is Vincent J. Cornell's Realm of the Saint.[26]

With respect to mysticism, again such accounts and experience are to be found both across civilizations as well as throughout history. A general summary of world mysticism is given in Geoffrey Parrinder's Mysticism in the World's Religions.[27] A more detailed treatment of world mysticism is Steven T. Katz's edited anthology Comparative Mysticism,[28] although Katz's constructivist approach to mystical interpretation is best balanced in consideration with Robert K.C. Forman's three edited volumes, The Problem of Pure Consciousness, The Innate Capacity and Mysticism, Mind, Consciousness.[29] As with the phenomenon of miracles, the phenomenon of mysticism, although comparatively rare, is nevertheless sufficiently common as to be resistant to ready dismissal, yet in its experiential implications it strikes directly at the roots of immanent closure, serving as it were as a chink in the wall of such a closure that nevertheless stands open to transcendence.

With respect to philosophical proofs or arguments for the existence of God, such proofs have satisfied many profound thinkers, but have never satisfied all, not even during earlier ages of faith. It is not in the nature of philosophical arguments, on God or any other topic, to compel universal assent, nor should this be looked for either as a reasonable goal or as a measure of efficacy or correctness. Nevertheless, the contemporary situation is remarkable in that there have never been so many or so well argued proofs for the existence of God, whether new articulations or defenses of old proofs found problematic, such as the modal formulation or Gödel's formulation of the ontological argument, or new proofs not previously conceived, such as various proofs based upon the nature of mathematics. Further, important arguments undermining the existence of God have been successfully countered, such as the free will defense against the argument from evil, or rendered problematic, such as the scientific issues raised with respect to cosmological fine-tuning or the origin of life, which act as strong pointers in support of the argument from design, quite apart from the Darwinian challenge to the argument from design with respect to living forms themselves. Further, individual arguments may be brought together to form a cumulative philosophic case considerably stronger than any single argument taken in isolation, a cumulative case that may well be judged far more compelling than any similar cumulative case against the existence of God. There is no one source that satisfactorily covers all these various arguments in both breadth and depth, but two good summaries are Peter Kreeft & Ronald K. Tacelli's "Twenty Arguments for the Existence of God"[30] and Alvin Plantinga's "Two Dozen (or so) Theistic Arguments."[31] A clear and careful articulation of Aquinas' principal arguments—the famous "Five Ways"— may be found in Edward Feser's *Aquinas*,[32] while a detailed treatment of more recent arguments is given in Robert J. Spitzer's *New Proofs for the Existence of God*.[33]

1 · B The Problem of the Historian

1. B. 1 The Smuggled Anti-Supernaturalism of Empiricism

The stance of immanent closure is closely bound up in practice with the epistemic assumption of empiricism, central to the philosophic underpinnings of natural science, but also carried over into other domains of inquiry, including the study of history. As a working assumption, empiricism has proven fruitful, but it nevertheless tends in practice to carry unwarranted metaphysical assumptions in its train, most notably that of naturalism or physicalism, which in turn implies an assumption of anti-supernaturalism, whether considered empirically or ontologically. The guiding assumption is that the supernatural is impossible to experience and in any case has no reality. This assumption, of course, is embedded in a particular intellectual history, that of the European Enlightenment paradigm, one historians themselves are as bound up in as moderns generally. As Craig S. Keener has noted:

> We typically ground our critique of supernatural phenomena in a modern Western worldview that we do not question, and then use those untested assumptions to posit an authoritative metanarrative or construal of reality.[34]

Similarly, C. Stephen Evans has observed:

> The claim that it is impossible for anyone to experience God or God's activity does not look as though it follows from any plausible version of empiricism. Rather, it reflects a priori convictions about the character of the divine and the relation of the divine to the natural world. Someone who insists that empirical religious knowledge is impossible seems to know a priori that religious knowledge has as its subject matter something that could not appear in space and time, or something that could not be recognized if it did. However,

such an a priori conviction does not stem from the genuinely empirical spirit, but reflects a rationalist mind-set.[35]

Further, as David Bentley Hart has argued:

> We may, obviously, as modern men and women, find certain of the fundamental convictions that our ancestors harbored curious and irrational; but this is not because we are somehow more advanced in our thinking than they were, even if we are aware of a greater number of scientific facts. We have simply adopted different conventions of thought and absorbed different prejudices, and so we interpret our experiences according to another set of basic beliefs—beliefs that may, for all we know, blind us to entire dimensions of reality.

> Certainly we moderns should not be too quick to congratulate ourselves, or to imagine ourselves as having embraced a more rational approach to the world, simply because we are less prone than were ancient persons to believe in miracles, or demons, or other supernatural agencies. We have no real rational warrant for deploring the "credulity" of the peoples of previous centuries toward the common basic assumptions of their times while implicitly celebrating ourselves for our own largely uncritical obedience to the common basic assumptions of our own.[36]

The procedure for the practice of such implicit anti-supernaturalism in the context of the secular study of religion has been aptly described by Peter L. Berger:

> The ideological interest that concerns me most is much more basic: It is the interest in the quasi-scientific legitimation of the avoidance of transcendence. My thesis is this: The functional approach to religion whatever the theoretical intentions of its authors, serves to provide quasi-scientific legitimations of a secularized world view. It achieves this purpose by an essentially simple cognitive procedure: The specificity of the religious phenomenon [*viz.* its transcendent character] is avoided by equating it with other phenomena.

The religious phenomenon is "flattened out." Finally, it is no longer perceived. Religion is absorbed into a night in which all cats are grey. The greyness is the secularized view of reality in which any manifestations of transcendence are, strictly speaking, meaningless, and therefore can only be dealt with in terms of social or psychological functions that can be understood without reference to transcendence.[37]

1. B. 2 The Incoherence of Secular Objectivity

One of the key claims underpinning the assumption of epistemic superiority on the part of the secular historian vis-à-vis the religious believer is that of objectivity. Specifically, the believer, by his faith commitment, is considered as lacking the impartial judgment necessary for proper scholarship. Such a claim of secular objectivity may, however, be challenged at multiple points. As an initial foray, given contemporary scholarly concerns to root out power masquerading in the guise of truth, a scripture—such as the Bible or Qur'ān—may indeed be read by a secular historian as an expression of ideology in the service of power. However, such a reading may be readily reversed to apply to the secular historian himself, who is himself hardly free from considerations of ideology, power or intellectual domination over the non-modern, non-Western "other". This is, after all, the meaning of "Orientalism" as has been documented by Edward Said with respect to Western historical criticism of the Qur'ān and of Western scholarly criticism of Islam more generally:

> I have not been able to discover any period in European or American history since the Middle Ages in which Islam was generally discussed or thought about outside a framework created by passion, prejudice, and political interests. This may not seem a surprising discovery, but included in it is the entire gamut of scholarly and scientific disciplines which, since the early nineteenth century, have either called themselves collectively the discipline of Orientalism or have

17

tried systematically to deal with the Orient.... Not that Orientalism is more biased than other social and humanistic sciences; it is simply as ideological and as contaminated by the world as other disciplines. The main difference is that Orientalist scholars have tended to use their standing as experts to deny—and sometimes even to cover—their deep-seated feelings about Islam with a language of authority whose purpose is to certify their "objectivity" and "scientific impartiality."[38]

More decisively, the stance of the historian, insofar as it claims to be "objective", amounts to a claim of standing outside of the historical process altogether, of rising above the immanent domain. But this is precisely what its own preconditions disallow, for the first act of historical criticism is to bar the door to transcendence. As such, its claim to objectivity is simply incoherent. As Leo Strauss has judged the matter:

> Historicism asserts that all human thoughts or beliefs are historical, and hence deservedly destined to perish; but historicism itself is a human thought; hence historicism can be of only temporary validity, or it cannot be simply true. To assert the historicist thesis means to doubt it and thus to transcend it.... Historicism thrives on the fact that it inconsistently exempts itself from its own verdict about all human thought.... We cannot see the historical character of "all" thought—that is, of all thought with the exception of the historicist insight and its implications—without transcending history, without grasping something trans-historical.[39]

Jon D. Levenson has noted similarly:

> Many will recognize these last remarks as an example of the exercise that Peter Berger has called "relativizing the relativizers." In the context at hand, it would be more accurately termed "suspecting the hermeneuts of suspicion." By posing the question of the modern interpreters' own place

in reality as they sketch it, one challenges them to justify their claim, express or implicit, of independence from the dynamics that they depict as ultimate. Might it be the case that the interpretation of religion as only a mystification of power arrangements, for example, is itself an item in a discourse of power in which a new group, supported by new social arrangements, asserts its hegemony?[40]

The unwarranted modern exemption from historical relativization has been highlighted by Peter L. Berger:

> I am not concerned for the moment with either the viability of the translation process or the empirical validity of the premise about modern man, but rather with a hidden *double standard*, which can be put quite simply: The past, out of which the tradition comes, is relativized in terms of this or that socio-historical analysis. The *present*, however, remains strangely immune from relativization.[41]

The assumption of relativization eventually acts as a kind of universal acid, undermining the position of the relativizer himself, as Berger has further observed:

> One (perhaps literally) redeeming feature of the sociological perspective is that relativizing analysis, in being pushed to its final consequence, bends back upon itself. The relativizers are relativized, the debunkers are debunked—indeed, relativization itself is somehow liquidated.[42]

The unraveling of the secular claim to objectivity in turn unravels the accompanying judgment that the observing outsider, with his supposed "impartiality" and "commitment to truth", is in a privileged position relative to the participating insider. Once this impartiality is unmasked as either illusory or incoherent, the privilege of the outsider stance is lost. As Jon D. Levenson has concluded:

> The belief that the real meaning of religious phenomena is available only to the outside observer is a secular analogue

19

to religious revelation. If so, then a system of thought like historicism which "exempts itself from its own verdict," is a secular equivalent to fundamentalism. For though it subjects all else to critique, it asserts axiomatically its own inviolability to critique. Demanding to be the norm by means of which truth and error are disclosed, this type of thinking, by definition, can never be in error.[43]

William A. Graham has similarly noted the inherent difficulty, if not practical impossibility, of such an objective stance in the specific context of Western Qur'ān scholarship:

Since the Enlightenment, non-Muslim Qur'ān study has come into its own as a part of more general Islamic studies within the modern university and its academic tradition. This tradition is in *theory* explicitly set apart from confessional presuppositions of any one religious tradition, its sole arbiter being human reason and its primary object knowledge that is (a) verifiable—at least within the limits of human reason—and (b) also accessible to anyone of any creed or ideology who agrees to submit to the strictures of reasoned and public inquiry and discussion. *Ideally*, this should mean freedom from all dogmatism, religious or otherwise. In *practice*, however it has proved to be most difficult to escape either religious or ideological bias on the one hand or, on the other, the naturalistic or even materialist delusion that by limiting discussion to purely external data of the sense world, one has dealt adequately with reality.[44]

1. B. 3 The Tenuousness of Secular Historical Judgment

Apart from the matters raised above, a critical additional point is that much secular historical judgment, even when pursued with great thoroughness and reasonable impartiality, remains tenuous, as historians will readily admit. As a point of reference, Peter Van Inwagen, in his review of the work of C. Stephen Evans,[45] cites, in the context of skeptical New Testament scholarship, the following problematic issues:

(1) "there is very little agreement" among such scholars;

(2) not all such scholars "arrive at unorthodox conclusions";

(3) "a really substantial proportion of the arguments the skeptics employ are very *bad* arguments";

(4) "the arguments of many of the skeptics have premises that are philosophical rather than historical";

(5) a general lack of literary judgment or perception regarding the quality of the texts studied; and

(6) "the community of skeptical critics is entirely naive and unself-critical as regards its own claims to objectivity."

Although there are many secular historical scholars studying the Qur'ān who have carried out valuable and significant work—a number of whom we liberally quote from—many of the same issues noted above may reasonably be observed to apply, *mutatis mutandis*, to this scholarly community as well:

(1) Certainly, the absence of any coherent collective view among this community—apart from the secular rejection of the revelatory status of the Qur'ān—has been evident for quite some time. Notably, often the sharpest criticism of a given scholarly position is not raised by Muslims, but by other such scholars.

(2) While there are a small but growing number of Muslim scholars of the Qur'ān in a Western context who accept the normative Islamic view regarding the revelatory status of the Qur'ān, a significantly larger body of non-Muslim scholars of the Qur'ān accept, at least provisionally, historical Muslim accounts regarding such foundational issues as the existence of Muhammad and his external role in communicating the Qur'ān, the historical context of various Qur'ānic suras or chapters and the codification of the Qur'ānic *muṣḥaf* or codex.

(3) Certainly, arguments are given by secular historical scholars that rest on thin or problematic evidence, often com-

bined with unwarranted conjecture, which may indeed be judged "bad". Explanations regarding the source and character of Muhammad's revelatory experiences, even from careful and fairly sympathetic scholars such as W. Montgomery Watt, tend to be particularly flimsy or dubious.

(4) Presuppositions or premises, such as rejecting miraculous accounts out of hand, which are essentially philosophical, are certainly very common, so much so that they are often taken for granted and simply asserted without comment or motivation.

(5) Given the esteem with which the literary quality of the Arabic Qur'ān has been held by general Muslim opinion, a lack of literary judgment or perception may be said to have hampered some, if certainly not all, Western scholars. With that said, there are a significant number of such scholars who have recognized and acknowledged the Qur'ān's literary qualities.

(6) Certainly, as treated in detail previously, there tends to be an unjustified conflation of "secular" and "objective", as if one necessarily implies the other.

Other observations regarding the character of secular historical scholarship on the Qur'ān that may also be raised include a tendency toward cynicism, rejection and disbelief with respect to Muslim historical sources, as well as a skewed overemphasis on tracing linkages to presumed Jewish or Christian source material. Four points also to be borne in mind are that, taken in a larger context, secular historical scholarship on the Qur'ān is, to a significant extent, a rider on the historical body of Islamic scholarship, to which it remains significantly indebted. Further, such secular historical scholarship, in contrast to its own self-understanding, is a comparatively marginal enterprise when taken in view with the long history of massive Islamic scholarly activity on the Qur'ān. Additionally, secular historical scholarship, by its relative removal in time and place from the context and event of the Qur'ānic disclosure, stands at multiple disadvantages of both knowledge and judgment in comparison to Islamic scholarship of centuries past. Finally, there is a sense in which the very nature of the Western scholarly enterprise sets it at odds with Islamic tradition, for if such scholars were, upon due consideration, to simply agree with historical Islamic understandings, they would by that very agreement largely annul their own relevance as scholars.

As a sampling of the various legitimate issues that may be raised with regard to the secular historical scholarship on the Qur'ān, one may recommend Muzaffar Iqbal's "The Qur'ān, Orientalism, and the Encyclopaedia of the Qur'ān,"[46] as well as Walid A. Saleh's "The Etymological Fallacy and Qur'ānic Studies"[47] and "A Piecemeal Qur'ān."[48]

1. B. 4 The Judgment of the Qur'ān on the Secular Historian

As previously noted, for the secular historical scholar studying the Qur'ān, concerns of academic objectivity or neutrality preclude acceptance of the Qur'ān as revelatory. However, such a stance runs hard against the Qur'ān's own demands upon its readers. For such a scholar, the Qur'ān may be taken seriously as an object of study, but must not be taken seriously as voicing a truth that might make demands upon him personally. As Mircea Eliade has more generally noted:

> ...the majority of the historians of religion defend themselves against the messages with which their documents are filled. This caution is understandable. One does not live with impunity in intimacy with "foreign" religious forms... But many historians of religion end by no longer taking seriously the spiritual worlds they study; they fall back on their personal religious faith, or they take refuge in a materialism or behaviorism impervious to every spiritual shock.[49]

Similarly, as Muzaffar Iqbal has more specifically observed:

... non-Muslim scholars in Western academia face a unique dilemma when approaching the Qur'ān: they cannot commit themselves to any position about the Divine origin of the Qur'ān because their professional obligation is to maintain an uncommitted detachment from the object of their study. Yet, in this case, the object itself makes it impossible to maintain such neutrality, for the Qur'ān demands that one must settle the fundamental issue of its authorship before any further interaction can occur. One must either accept or reject the Qur'ānic claim to be actual Divine Revelation. A corollary of whatever choice they make is their position regarding the Prophet. Acceptance of the Qur'ān as Divine Revelation simultaneously entails the acceptance of Prophet Muhammad as the final Messenger of Allah. If they reject the Qur'ānic claim, they simultaneously reject his prophethood and thereby find themselves in the difficult position of questioning his honesty and truthfulness—something that polemical writers have done for centuries. This dilemma has been recognized by a number of academic scholars along with the admission that no alternative solutions are available.[50]

As Jonathan A. C. Brown has similarly commented:

> What we must admit before any further discussion is that, because a book does not assume that God directly intervenes in human events [and] that Muhammad was a prophet... then what it really assumes is that God does *not* directly interfere in historical events [and] that Muhammad was *just a man*....[51]

Muḥammad Muṣṭafā al-Aʿẓamī has, rather more pointedly, concurred:

> Anyone writing about Islam must initially decide whether or not he believes in Muhammad as a prophet. Scholars who acknowledge him as a genuine messenger, the noblest of all prophets, enjoy an incredible library of *Ḥadīth* and divine revelations from which to draw their inspiration. By necessity they will share innumerable similarities, even total agreement on fundamental issues; whatever minor variations arise due

to shifting circumstances are entirely natural and human. Those refusing this viewpoint however, must by extension see Muhammad as a deluded madman or a liar bearing false claims of prophethood. This is the adopted stance of all non-Muslim scholars, through which their efforts are filtered: if they did not set out to prove Muhammad's dishonesty or the Qur'ān's fallacy, what would hinder them from accepting Islam?[52]

The Qur'ān's own perspective on such a reader is most often described in a language of epistemic futility. The one who rejects the message suffers from a deafness, a blindness, a heart that is hardened or veiled from understanding or accepting the truth. Again, as Muzaffar Iqbal has judged:

> The Qur'ān declares that Allah has sealed the hearts and the hearings of those who do not believe and *over their eyes is a veil* (Qur'ān, 2:7); and *there are among them such as [seem to] listen to thee [O Prophet], but over their hearts We have laid veils which prevent them from grasping the truth, and into their ears, deafness* (Qur'ān, 6:25); and *whenever you recite the Qur'ān, We place an invisible barrier between you and those who do not believe in the Hereafter; for, over their hearts We have laid veils which prevent them from grasping it, and into their ears, deafness* (Qur'ān, 17:45). One cannot discount this spiritual deprivation when considering scholarship on the Qur'ān, for spiritual receptivity is a *sine qua non* for drinking from this font of guidance and partaking of even a ray from this ocean of light.[53]

This highlights a distinction between modern and traditional assumptions regarding the state of one who engages in scholarship and the nature of the scholarship so produced. Iqbal stresses the secular assumption, "that there is no real relation between the spiritual state of a person writing an encyclopedic article and his or her intellectual output,"[54] in order to refute it. The point he makes is as transparent as it is profound. As William C. Chittick has similarly observed, the guiding frame and assumptions with which one approaches the text dictate to a very large extent what one receives from it:

> I chose to talk about the Koran as a "mirror" because I wanted to stress the role of the interpreter in understanding scripture. The fact that people see the Koran through their own specific lenses is especially clear when one surveys the vast number of Koranic commentaries written over the centuries—not to mention the critiques and studies written by non-Muslims. Jurists have found in the Koran a book of law, theologians see all sorts of God-talk, philosophers find the guidelines for wisdom and virtue, linguists uncover fascinating intricacies of Arabic grammar, biologists find theories of life. As for Western scholarship, nothing is more obvious than that scholars reach different conclusions on the basis of diverse premises and prejudices.[55]

The Qur'ān speaks of itself as a book that "none but the purified shall touch," [56: 79] which raises a very salient consideration, one common to every tradition, whether Buddhist, Hindu, Jewish, Christian, Islamic or Platonic—that of the necessity of purification as an inescapable initial stage of intellectual engagement. As Mark Anderson has noted, "The greatest of the ancient and medieval metaphysicians taught that metaphysical knowledge is accessible only to those who practice purification."[56] Such a necessity has been entirely lost sight of, for the ontological collapse to materiality that characterized the onset of modernity went hand in hand with an epistemic collapse regarding the prerequisites of knowledge. As Anderson has further noted:

> The ascendancy of modern science, of empiricism on one side and "the method" on the other, coincides with the rejection— or rather the neglect and forgetting—of purification as a prerequisite to knowledge. At the onset of modernity the search for knowledge was turned over to the senses and technique; the purificatory virtues dropped out. If only the

physical is knowable, as long as the body is functioning properly one may ignore the soul. Even a criminal can operate a microscope.[57]

If the reader is profanized, then the Book is profanized; conversely, if the reader is sacralized, then the Book is sacralized. The one reads the Qur'ān as immanent deception; the other reads the Qur'ān as transcendent Disclosure. The reader finds what his state conditions and enables him to find.

2

The Qur'ān and its Context

2 · A   Social Considerations

2. A. 1   Codification and Preservation

Quite apart from the question of whether the Qur'ān is the word of God or of Muhammad, the question must also be addressed as to whether the Qur'ān as we have it can be reliably traced to Muhammad's immediate milieu. Such a concern turns upon two further considerations: first, whether the text of the Qur'ān was codified, as Muslim history records, within a few years of the death of the Prophet, culminating in the 'Uthmānic recension; second, whether the codified text was accurately transmitted through the course of subsequent history. Turning to this first consideration, a number of Western "revisionist" scholars have rejected Muslim history, favoring instead the view of a late codification of Qur'ān, some centuries after the death of the Prophet. This position, always a minority view, has, more recently, been significantly curtailed.

Whether the Qur'ān was in fact the revelation it claimed to be, there is every reason to believe that Muhammad's followers, particularly those companions closest to him, were deeply sincere in their belief that the Qur'ān was exactly what it and Muhammad claimed. Concomitant conclusions regarding their conduct in the face of this conviction naturally follow. Those in political authority after the death of Prophet, most

significantly Abū Bakr and 'Uthmān, were pious individuals
of high reputation, as were those, most significantly Zayd ibn
Thābit, charged with the codification of the Qur'ānic text. To
suggest, particularly from a vast historical distance with all
the uncertainties this entails, the possibility of gross, or even
indeed marginal, mishandling of what they understood to be
the very word of God, can only strike one as highly improbable
on psychological grounds alone. As Alan Jones has argued:

> Questions are asked by non-Muslims about the recension that
> are answered for a Sunnī Muslim by his faith. The two on
> which there is greatest speculation are whether the Qur'ān,
> as we have it in 'Uthmān's recension, is complete, and how
> much the editors were responsible for the arrangement of
> material within the suras. In each case the frank answer is
> that we do not know; the varying views of orientalists are a
> mixture of prejudice and speculation. As far as completeness
> is concerned, there is no reason to think that anything
> important has gone astray, unless one accepts the story of Abū
> Mūsā at its face value. Bell states the position very reasonably
> when he says that the fact that varying, and sometimes even
> contradictory, deliverances have been preserved is strong
> proof that there was no deliberate suppression, and that the
> editors acted in good faith... the good faith of the editors,
> in its fullest sense, is a factor that should not be overlooked.
> They were god-fearing men who had known the inspiration
> of the Prophet. There can be little doubt that their desire
> in preparing the recension would have been to serve Allah
> before all else. Such an attitude would be a strong incentive
> to them to exercise care and caution in their revision.[58]

As a further line of testimony to the historical reality of the
Qur'ānic revelation in the context of Muhammad's immediate
milieu, certain Western historical scholars—having previously
given an excess of consideration to contemporaneous non-
Muslim sources in an attempt to discredit Muslim historical
accounts—have, in the face of additional such source materi-

als, abandoned this view.[59] In point of fact, such non-Muslim sources are, within the limitations of their own perspectives, frequently in general agreement with Islamic historical understanding. Robert Hoyland, in summarizing his extensive research in this area, has argued:

> Throughout this book I have striven to bring out the parallels and similarities between the reports of Muslim and non-Muslim witnesses. The reason for this approach is that it seems to me a strong argument in favor of the latter that they do frequently coincide with what is said by the former. If both the Muslim and non-Muslim sources give a false picture of events, how are we to explain that they both give the same false picture? Many of the non-Muslim sources are demonstrably early, so borrowing or later reworking could certainly not account for all cases of agreement. And as van Ess states, "we should expect that he ('an observer from outside') tried to describe the phenomenon (of Islam) with his own categories," so it cannot be that the concord is attributable to shared presuppositions. The answer must be either that they are giving independent testimony or, as is more common, that they are interdependent, but in which case the picture, whether false or not, is as old as the non-Muslim source presenting it.[60]

Also of considerable significance, radiocarbon dating on a number of early Qur'ān samples has confirmed dating in broad agreement with historical Islamic accounts. Of these, the most significant work has been done on the "Ṣanʿāʾ 1" early Qur'ānic palimpsest found in the Great Mosque of Sana'a in Yemen.[61] The under-layer of Qur'ānic writing of the palimpsest has been radiocarbon dated and judged to be more than 95% likely to have originated in the period 578–669 AD. More recently, two Qur'ān manuscript fragments in library holdings in the University of Tübingen and the University of Birmingham have been radiocarbon dated and judged to be more than 95% likely to have respectively originated in the periods 649–675 AD and 568–645 AD.[62] According to Islamic tradition, the death of Muhammad is given as 632 AD, with the dissemination of the 'Uthmānic codex of the Qur'ān dated to the period 644–650 AD. All of these datings are, within the broad range of such dating, relatively close to one another, with the Birmingham manuscript, the oldest dated, judged with more than 95% accuracy to have been produced within 13 years of the Prophet's death.

Another indication of the early formation and subsequent faithful preservation of the Qur'ānic codex is the lack of evidence for redaction of the text in light of the Muslim conquests in the period following the death of the Prophet. As F. E. Peters has noted:

> As has already been said, there was no Easter for the Muslims—Muhammad died of natural causes in AD 632 and by all reports still rests in his tomb in the mosque at Medina—but the enormous and astonishing expansion of Islam, which was unmistakably underway when the Qur'ān was collected into its final form sometime about 650, is an Islamic event of similar if not identical redactional magnitude to the Christians' Easter. If the almost miraculous success of the movement he initiated did not change the Muslims' essential regard for Muhammad, who was after all only a man, it could certainly have cast a different light on his version of God's message. However, we find no trace of this in the Qur'ān, no signs that its "good news" was "redacted" in the afterglow of an astonishing politico-military authentication of its religious truths.[63]

Yet another indication of the early formation and faithful preservation of the Qur'ānic codex is the uniformity of Qur'ānic copies across the Islamic word, both in terms of a lack of regional variations at the time of early Muslim expansion as well as thereafter, but also a lack of variations among rival early Muslim groups. In this latter regard François De Blois has noted:

Although the surviving Muslim sects (the Shī'ites, Khārijites, and those who eventually came to be known as Sunnites) separated from each other within a decade of the death of Muhammad, they all agree on the content of the Qur'ānic canon.[64]

William Muir had made the same point long before:

> There has never been anything other than one Qur'ān for every faction, however implacable; and this unanimous usage of the same scripture accepted by all up to the present day is one of the unchallengeable proofs of the trustworthiness of the text which we possess, and which goes right back to the unfortunate caliph ['Uthmān, who was assassinated].[65]

Even assuming early codification of the Qur'ānic text, the question of the transmission of the Qur'ān through the course of history must further be addressed. In this regard, one aspect of the Qur'ān's historical preservation and transmission that is at once unusual and remarkable, particularly in terms of scale, is the mass memorization of the Qur'ān from generation to generation, down to the present day. The Qur'ān has never just been preserved in written form, but parallel with this has also been preserved in the hearts of men and women. As Kenneth Cragg has reminded:

> ... this phenomenon of Qur'ānic recital means that the text has traversed the centuries in an unbroken living sequence of devotion. It cannot, therefore, be handled as an antiquarian thing, nor as a historical document out of a distant past. The fact of "ḥifẓ" (Qur'ānic memorization) has made the Qur'ān a present possession through all the lapse of Muslim time and given it a human currency in every generation, never allowing its relegation to a bare authority for reference alone.[66]

In this respect, and apart from the significance of the general memorization of the Qur'ān, the chains of transmission (*isnād*) of formal Qur'ān reciters, with their respective certifications (*ijāza*) from one generation of masters to the next, extending back in time to the Prophet and his companions, form a significant record of uninterrupted, verified transmission from the beginning of Islamic history to the present day.[67]

The Qur'ān has thus enjoyed a widespread dual transmission, at once written and oral, one which has enabled an effective redundancy that has contributed to the accuracy of the transmitted Qur'ān. As Adrian Brocket has weighed:

> If the Qur'ān had been transmitted only orally for the first century, sizeable variations between texts such as are seen in the *Ḥadīth* and pre-Islamic poetry would be found, and if it had been transmitted only in writing, sizeable variations such as in the different transmission of the original document of the Constitution of Medina would be found. But neither is the case with the Qur'ān. There must have been a parallel written transmission limiting variation in the oral transmission to the graphic form, side by side with a parallel oral transmission preserving the written transmission from corruption.[68]

On the whole, textual variants in Qur'ān manuscripts, when they have appeared at all, have been minor, rarely, if ever, affecting the meaning of the text. A significant representative example is that of the early Sana'a fragments mentioned above. As Gerd Puin has remarked:

> The important thing... is that these Yemeni Qur'ānic fragments do not differ from those found in museums and libraries elsewhere, with the exception of details that do not touch the Qur'ān itself, but are rather differences in the way words are spelled.[69]

More generally, John Wansbrough has noted: "Of genuinely textual variants exhibiting material deviation from the canonical text of revelation, such as are available for Hebrew and Christian scripture, there are none."[70] Similarly, François De Blois has observed:

> Within the Qur'ānic canon, there are no really substantial

textual variants. The so-called "reading variants" (*qirā'āt*) recorded in medieval writings on Qur'ānic sciences are for the most part mere graphic variants, that is, different spellings of the same recited texts, and even the very few true textual variants hardly ever make any difference in the content of the book. This is equally true of the ancient Qur'ān fragments discovered in Ṣanʿā'... I have already suggested elsewhere that the virtual absence of real textual variants in the Qur'ān is the result of the fact that the transmission of the Qur'ān has always been primarily through oral rather than through written tradition.[71]

In reviewing these and other lines of argument, Angelika Neuwirth has noted:

> As a whole, however, the theories of the so-called skeptic or revisionist scholars who, arguing historically, make a radical break with the transmitted picture of Islamic origins, shifting them in both time and place from the seventh to the eighth or ninth century and from the Arabian peninsula to the Fertile Crescent, have by now been discarded, though many of their critical observations remain challenging and still call for investigation. New findings of Qur'ānic text fragments, moreover, can be adduced to affirm rather than call into question the traditional picture of the Qur'ān as an early fixed text composed of the *sūrah*s we have. Nor have scholars trying to deconstruct that image through linguistic arguments succeeded in seriously discrediting the genuineness of the Qur'ān as we know it.[72]

Similarly, M. A. S. Abdel Haleem has argued on multiple grounds:

> I am convinced that the Qur'ān, as we know it now, is exactly the same as the Prophet recited and I base this conviction on several arguments.

> First of all we have to consider the length of Muhammad's prophethood. Jesus only had two and a half years to complete

his mission but Muhammad was there for twenty three years. In the last ten years he had thousands of companions and he was with them every day in the mosque, reciting the verses to them and making sure they read it correctly.

Secondly, in the Arab culture of those days, everything was learned by heart. Their genealogy, their history, their poetry, and so on, they memorized it all. And the Qur'ān is only about five hundred pages. If we divide this over twenty three years, two or three pages each month, then it becomes clear that it's really not beyond people's capacity to learn the Qur'ān by heart.

Thirdly, we have to keep in mind that people believed that it was the word of God. Because people who believe it's the word of God will exert great efforts in learning it properly. If you think how the first Muslims sacrificed themselves completely for the cause, it is difficult for me to imagine that they would deliberately change the words or concoct certain adaptations. That does not make sense. It makes a lot more sense to think that they would go to great lengths to retain the words exactly like the Prophet had told them as they still do, at all ages, Arabic speakers and other Muslims.

On top of this, the Qur'ān was put into writing on sundry materials during the lifetime of the Prophet. Already fourteen months after he died, a situation arose where everything had to be brought together and written down in one volume. Then, twenty years later, that first volume was copied and verified and six more copies were made and nobody has ever dared to change anything in those texts. Even the orthography has retained peculiarities which no longer exist in Arabic writing but these have not been changed.

Lastly we shouldn't forget that on top of this, the Qur'ān, unlike all other scriptures, was always protected right from the beginning, by the heads of state, as some Western scholars have pointed out. So its integrity was always closely guarded by those in power.

As you notice, I don't use any theological arguments. When I teach I don't use any theological arguments either, because my students aren't only Muslims. Sometimes they're Jewish, Christian, Hindu or Buddhist. I am not a theologian or a preacher; I am an academic and I deal with language, style and translation, so it's not my job to convince people of my faith.[73]

2. A. 2 Lack of Cultural Precedent

Turning to the question of the authorship of the Qur'ān itself, a number of distinct issues may be brought under consideration. Among these, the question of cultural precedent looms large, for the Qur'ān stands as a massive discontinuity in respect to precedent cultural elements that might conceivably have informed it and given it shape. While the Qur'ān may make use of such elements, it is, ultimately, irreducible to them. As Angelika Neuwirth has candidly observed:

> ... no one has succeeded, this is right... I really think that the Qur'ān has even brought Western researchers embarrassment, who weren't able to clarify how suddenly in an environment where there were not any appreciable written texts, appeared the Qur'ān with its richness of ideas and its magnificent wordings.[74]

There is little in pre-Islamic Arabic oral culture—pre-Islamic written culture being effectively nonexistent—that might serve as a formative precedent for the Qur'ān. On the contrary, what characterizes the Qur'ān as a cultural phenomenon for the Arabs of the time is precisely its uniqueness—they had never seen anything like it in their cultural experience, and it appeared, as it were, out of nowhere, without recognizable cultural precedent. As F. E. Peters has noted:

> The Qur'ān therefore stands isolated like an immense composite rock jutting forth from a desolate sea, a stony eminence

with few marks upon it to suggest how or why it appeared in this watery desert.[75]

Hans Küng has similarly commented upon the profound discontinuity of the message brought by Muhammad:

> Muhammad—to be more precise, the Qur'ān—obviously constitutes an epochal turning point in the history of the Arab peoples: Muhammad is discontinuity in person, an ultimately irreducible figure, who cannot be simply derived from what preceded him, but stands radically apart from it as he, with the Qur'ān, establishes permanent new standards. In that respect, Muhammad and the Qur'ān represent a decisive break, a departure from the past, a shift toward a new future.[76]

2. A. 3 Decisiveness of Social Impact

Another issue that may be brought to bear is that of social impact, for the Qur'ān was to utterly transform the pagan Arab society it informed, at once addressing and solving real social iniquities and impasses while turning it from a crude paganism to the purest monotheism within a single generation. As W. Montgomery Watt has noted:

> Whatever our theological position, we must in my opinion regard the Qur'ānic *kerygma* [proclamation] as a creative irruption into the Meccan situation. There were certainly problems to be solved, there were tensions from which men sought relief, but it was impossible by mere ratiocination, by logical thinking, to pass from these problems and tensions to the Qur'ānic *kerygma*.[77]

Further, the spread of the Qur'ānic message and the faith it inspired across a vast region spanning from Andalusia to China within a few decades of the death of Muhammad, the centuries-long permanence with which that message took root, and the civilizational achievements which were to directly follow, all stand in remarkable testimony to the profound effect of the Qur'ān. As Frithjof Schuon has remarked:

> The "Muslim miracle" was not only the lightning-like expansion followed by the adamantine stability of the new religion, but also the transforming of a people as passional and undisciplined as the ancient Arabs into the vehicle of the final religion and of one of the great civilizations of mankind.[78]

2. A. 4 Generation of Virtue and Sanctity

The Qur'ānic message has been astonishingly fecund in the course of fourteen centuries of Islamic history. One of the most significant measures of this fecundity is the impressive number of sanctified individuals—friends of God (*awliyā' Allāh*)—whose spiritual qualities stand in witness to the Qur'ān's transformative influence. A noteworthy record of such is Muḥyī al-Dīn ibn al-'Arabī's *Rūḥ al-Quds*,[79] which documents case after case of quite ordinary individuals possessed of extraordinary sanctity, a sanctity made possible through the Qur'ānic message and accompanying ambiance. Similarly, one might mention Farīd al-Dīn 'Aṭṭār's *Tadhkirat al-Awliyā'*,[80] which provides a further record of the wide-ranging extent of Islamic sanctity. A recent addition to such literature documenting a number of remarkable contemporary examples of Islamic sanctity is Michael Sugich's *Signs on the Horizons*.[81] In contrast, texts of strictly human creation are, needless to say, not known for the generation of such fruits. As Martin Lings has emphasized:

> We must not forget that those non-Muslims who have made an objective study of comparative religion are unanimous in their judgment that *no* religion has produced saints greater than the saints of Islam: and this, for those who are capable of seeing it, is an altogether self-sufficient proof, which needs to be supplemented by no other evidence whatsoever.[82]

بِسۡمِ اللهِ الرَّحۡمٰنِ الرَّحِيۡمِ

اللّٰهُ لَاۤ اِلٰهَ اِلَّا هُوَ ۚ اَلۡحَیُّ الۡقَیُّوۡمُ ۚ۬

لَا تَاۡخُذُهٗ سِنَةٌ وَّلَا نَوۡمٌ ؕ

لَهٗ مَا فِی السَّمٰوٰتِ وَمَا فِی الۡاَرۡضِ ؕ

مَنۡ ذَا الَّذِیۡ یَشۡفَعُ عِنۡدَهٗۤ اِلَّا بِاِذۡنِهٖ ؕ

یَعۡلَمُ مَا بَیۡنَ اَیۡدِیۡهِمۡ وَمَا خَلۡفَهُمۡ ۚ

وَلَا یُحِیۡطُوۡنَ بِشَیۡءٍ مِّنۡ عِلۡمِهٖۤ اِلَّا بِمَا شَآءَ ۚ

وَسِعَ کُرۡسِیُّهُ السَّمٰوٰتِ وَالۡاَرۡضَ ۚ

وَلَا یَـُٔوۡدُهٗ حِفۡظُهُمَا ۚ وَهُوَ الۡعَلِیُّ الۡعَظِیۡمُ

صَدَقَ اللّٰهُ الۡعَظِیۡمُ

SURAH AL-BAQARAH, 2:255, THE "VERSE OF THE THRONE"

W. Montgomery Watt, whose position on the revelatory status of the Qur'ān was to gradually alter in its favor over the course of his long scholarly career, has similarly concurred:

> Personally I am convinced that Muhammad was sincere in believing that what came to him as revelation (*waḥy*) was not the product of conscious thought on his part. I consider that Muhammad was truly a Prophet, and think that we Christians should admit this on the basis of the Christian principle that "by their fruits you will know them," since through the centuries Islam has produced many upright and saintly people. If he is a prophet, too, then in accordance with the Christian doctrine that the Holy Spirit spoke by the prophets, the Qur'ān may be accepted as of divine origin.[83]

2. A. 5 Generation of Beauty of Forms

Just as the widespread presence of sanctity, or "beauty of soul," presents one kind of strongly suggestive argument, so the widespread presence of sacred art, or "beauty of form," presents another. In this respect, it is telling that the most typical Islamic word for spiritual excellence, *iḥsān*, precisely connotes "doing what is beautiful" or "making beautiful". This profusion of formal beauty in the context of multiple Islamic civilizations has been staggering. With regard to the beauty of forms, perhaps the most evident examples are architectural achievements such as the Alhambra in Granada, the Dome of the Rock in Jerusalem, the Süleymaniye Mosque in Istanbul, the Shah Mosque in Isfahan and the Taj Mahal in Agra. While each of these structures displays its own ethnic genius—Moorish, Syrian, Ottoman, Persian and Mughal, respectively—they are nevertheless collectively marked by a lucidity, serenity and harmony that is distinctively Islamic in inspiration and character. The concern with beauty of forms in traditional Islam extends to every domain of cultural expression, from Qur'ānic recitation and calligraphy, geometrical ornament and arabesque, the art of the book and miniature, poetry and music, continuing down to the most humble items of everyday use, including the art of dress and of the carpet.

Formal beauty, particularly of a sacred character, is a necessary marker of the truth and completeness of a given religious tradition, one that bears its own evident testimony. As Martin Lings has articulated:

> Sacred art is not a human invention: it is a divinely inspired crystallization of the ideal that its religion represents. To stand in front of one of the great mosques can be an experience that could change a man's life. Few indeed are those tongues which could achieve an eloquence for Islam comparable with the eloquent silence of the Taj Mahal for example, or the mosques of Persia, Turkey, Egypt and Morocco; and when the Arabs were driven out of Spain, they left behind them an Islam in stone which still has power to penetrate the soul to depths of which it was hitherto unconscious.[84]

The particular "genius" of the sacred art of Islam, in leading the soul from multiplicity to unity, has been clarified by Titus Burckhardt:

> In Islam the Divine Art—and according to the Koran God is "artist" (*muṣawwir*)—is in the first place the manifestation of the Divine Unity in the beauty and regularity of the cosmos. Unity is reflected in the harmony of the multiple, in order and in equilibrium; beauty has all these aspects within itself. To start from the beauty of the world and arrive at Unity—that is wisdom. For this reason Islamic thought necessarily attaches art to wisdom; in the eyes of a Muslim, art is essentially founded on wisdom, or on science, the function of science being the formulation of wisdom in temporal terms. The purpose of art is to enable the human environment, the world in so far as it is molded by man, to participate in the order that manifests most directly the Divine Unity. Art clarifies the

world; it helps the spirit to detach itself from the disturbing multitude of things so that it may climb again towards the Infinite Unity.[85]

2 · B   Doctrinal Considerations

2. B. 1   Doctrinal Self-Evidence

There are fundamental aspects of Qur'ānic doctrine, the *Shahādah* preeminent among these, which escape the question of historicist empiricism altogether.[86] The first half of the foundational creedal statement of the *Shahādah*, "no god but God," is both a matter of revelatory instruction and of direct and immediate insight, as the Islamic intellectual tradition has consistently held. As William C. Chittick has clarified:

> In Arabic, the statement "There is no god but God" is called *kalimat al-tawḥīd*, "the sentence asserting unity"—that is, the unity of God. The Koran presents *tawḥīd* as a self-evident truth lying at the heart of every prophetic message. The first of the 124,000 prophets God sent was Adam, and the last was Muhammad. The Koran tells us that the function of all prophets is to "remind" (*dhikr, tadhkira*) people of *tawḥīd*. To speak of a "reminder" is to say that there is nothing new or innovative about *tawḥīd*. People already know that God is one, which is to say that they have an innate intuition that reality is coherent, integrated, and whole. In Koranic terms, this knowledge pertains to the original human nature (*fiṭra*), that is, to the intelligence and self-awareness that distinguish human beings from other creatures. Hence, the first function of the prophets is to help people recognize—that is, to *re*-cognize—what they already know. Here again, Plato provides a parallel with his notion of reminiscence.
>
> *Tawḥīd* is utterly basic to the Islamic worldview and is the constant point of reference for the intellectual tradition.

Philosophers take it for granted, even if they devote many volumes to explaining why it must be so and why it underlies all true knowledge. For their part, the Sufis also take *tawḥīd* for granted and, in their theoretical works, speak incessantly of the manner in which God's unity determines the nature of things.

When we look at the traditional understanding of the formula of *tawḥīd*: "There is no god but God", we realize that there is nothing specifically "Islamic" about it. It is an unremarkable statement about the universe, much as if we were to say: "The sky is up, the earth is down". Any rational person knows that reality is coherent, ordered, and somehow unified, and this knowledge lies behind every attempt to make sense of the world and the human situation. This is to say that the truth of *tawḥīd* is universal. It has nothing to do with the historical or cosmic situation. Reality is as it is; the "universe" is in fact unified, as the word itself reminds us.[87]

This foundational insight has been grasped and expressed in some form or another in every tradition apart from secular modernity. As Mircea Eliade has noted, "All authentic religious experience implies a desperate effort to penetrate to the root of things, the ultimate reality."[88] Similarly, as Frederick Copleston has confirmed, "the metaphysics of the One and the Many has often been associated or connected with religion."[89] The second half of the creedal statement of the *Shahādah*, "Muhammad is the messenger of God," contingently follows on this truth of the first, for if God may be directly seen to uniquely *be*, then Muhammad, by virtue of having communicated this same understanding through the Qur'ān, has thereby served as the vital intermediary for the revelatory confirmation of this immediate intellectual truth.

2.B.2 Universality of Vision

Just as the essentialist metaphysics of the first half of the *Shahā-dah* is indicative of the real as ultimate, so in a complementary way the understanding of prophethood inherent in the second half of the *Shahādah* is indicative of the real as universal, for Muhammad is called "the messenger of God," but is in no way understood as being unique in such a role. As Nasr Abu Zayd has emphasized:

> As a Message, Islam, according to the Qur'ān, is not a new religion brought down to Muhammad to preach to the Arabs, but essentially it is the same message preached by all the prophets since the creation of the world. "The religion God has established for you is the same religion as that which He enjoined on Noah, as it is also the same We enjoined on Abraham, Moses and Jesus" [42: 13]. "We have revealed to you the same We sent to Noah and the Messengers after him; We revealed to Abraham, Ishmael, Isaac, Jacob and the Tribes, to Jesus, Job, Jonah, Aaron and Solomon, and to David We gave the Psalms" [4: 163–4]. It is, therefore, inferred that all the prophets are considered as Muslims in the Qur'ān [cf. 6: 163; 7: 143; 10: 72, 84, 90; 27: 31, 38, 42, 91; 39: 12; 46: 15 etc...].[90]

Precisely because the Qur'ān reflects an explicit universality of religions,[91] in which there have been many revelations sent to many prophets, there is no additional requirement that other revelations also be false for the Qur'ānic revelation to be true. This has the particular effect of strengthening the revelatory claim of the Qur'ān in comparison to more exclusivist truth claims. As Ernest McClain has noted:

> *Islām* means *submission* to God, not to Muhammad or the Mullas (*'ulamā'*, scholars of theology), and from the beginning to the end of time whoever lives in submission to God is *Muslim* with no parochial limits of place or race. Contrast this generosity with Jewish exclusiveness, for instance, or with Christian bewilderment as to how to handle the paradisiacal immortal-

ity of a hero like Plato, born too soon to have been "saved" by Christ, yet the essential foundation for Christian theology. For those who follow the way of Muhammad, "Abraham was not a Jew nor yet a Christian" [3: 67], but a Muslim—for he submitted to God. Christ is a Muslim. His Apostles are Muslim [5: 114]. Christianity cannot compete with such catholicity and Judaism never aspired to. In any purely spiritual confrontation, Jewish and Christian self-identity may have to surrender to Islam; its self-defining terms are broader. The theological reductionism of Muhammad's monotheism is extreme. He aimed for the ultimate simplicity. His "Book that makes things clear" may have achieved the ultimate monotheistic generality, and in contests of ideas the particular loses to the general.[92]

2. B. 3 Completeness of Discourse

Although by no means immediately evident, yet another consideration in support of the Qur'ān's revelatory status is the comprehensiveness of its discourse. This has been brought out perhaps most clearly in Abū Ḥāmid al-Ghazālī's forty volume *magnum opus*, the *Iḥyā' 'Ulūm al-Dīn*, and has been particularly noted in this regard by T. J. Winter: "The completeness of the vision of the Qur'ān that Imam al-Ghazālī displays in the *Iḥyā'* is an objective argument for the truth of the revelation."[93] Commenting further, he has argued:

> One of the disclosures that the *Iḥyā'* provides is the clearest disclosure that I've come across of the miraculous completeness of the Qur'ān's religious discourse. That he [al-Ghazālī] travels through so much territory. There is no vice and no virtue, no issue of human life, no question of the *'ibādāt* [forms of worship], no point of doctrine that he does not cover, guided always by the principle of sorting out what is essential from what is superficial, by his concern for *ākhirah* [the afterlife]. Not one of those territories that he crosses is not linked fundamentally to a whole raft of Qur'ānic quotations.

46

"We have not left anything out of the book" [Qur'ān 6: 38], and the *Iḥyā' 'Ulūm al-Dīn* really is the great proof of that. The *Iḥyā' 'Ulūm al-Dīn* demonstrates to skeptics, as no other book of my acquaintance has done, the truth of the Qur'ān's claim not to have missed anything. And this is, I think, a stimulating challenge to a certain type of secular, historiographic put-down of our founding document, viewing it in terms of a series of half-discernible influences—Syriac Christianity and Medinan Rabbinic Judaism and Arabian tribal law—and the speculations that they offer can be no more than speculations because they don't have the immediately precedent texts to demonstrate influence. But that thesis surely collapses spectacularly when we look at Imam al-Ghazālī's take on the Qur'ānic architecture, demonstrating the extraordinary, miraculous, profound completeness of Allah's book.[94]

2. B. 4 Coordination with Classical Philosophic Theism

Classical theism, the common philosophical understanding of God developed by Greek, Christian, Jewish and Islamic metaphysicians, developed from the axiomatic intuition of God as the ultimate reality. The conception of God philosophically derived from this foundational perception includes the following aspects or properties: unity, simplicity, necessity, complete independence, self-sufficiency, incorporeality, eternality, immutability, omnipresence, perfection of intellect, perfection of will.[95] Such a conception, for all its metaphysical depth and philosophical richness, addresses only a narrow slice of the attributes and character of the God of revelation, whether—in the case of the Abrahamic religions—of the Torah, New Testament or Qur'ān. Nevertheless, its coherence and philosophical sophistication have rendered classical theism, "the mainstream understanding of the divine nature through most of the history both of philosophical theology and of the main monotheistic religions," as Edward Feser has noted.[96]

From a specifically Islamic perspective, it may be argued

that the understanding of God as conceived under classical theism resonates most closely with that of God as conceived in Islamic terms, not only in light of the general properties articulated under classical theism, which find close agreement, but also more particularly in light of the two critical properties of unity and universality which are emphasized with great vigor and clarity under Islam. Whereas Yahweh is predominantly conceived as the god specifically of the Jewish people, Allāh, as presented in the Qur'ān, can in no way be conceived as the god of the Arabs, but rather is God of all. Whereas God as conceived by Christian theologians is Trinitarian, thereby bringing the multiplicity of the Trinity into the very core of Divinity, such that a precedent and underlying unity would be problematically denied, the God of the Qur'ān is most emphatically One.

There is another aspect in which classical theism—what David Conway has termed "the classical conception of philosophy"—also closely harmonizes with the Islamic tradition. In summarizing this classical conception, Conway has stated:

> This conception may be summarized in the form of three theses which were assented to by all philosophers who espoused this conception of their subject. The first thesis is that *the goal of philosophy is the acquisition of* sophia *or theoretical wisdom*, where this is understood as consisting of a knowledge of why the world exists and has the broad form it does. The second thesis is that *the world is the handiwork of a supreme, omnipotent, and omniscient intelligence, or God, who created it in order that its rational inhabitants be led by employing their rational intellects to a knowledge of their Creator, and thereby be able to join God in the activity of* theoria, *understood as the contemplation of God*. The third thesis is that *it is in the activity of* theoria, *so understood, that supreme human happiness consists.*[97]

The activity of *theoria*, or the contemplation of God, bears a close parallel with the conjoined Islamic spiritual practices of *dhikr* and *fikr*, of invocation and remembrance combined with meditation and contemplation, which together fix and concentrate the mind upon God.

Finally, the Islamic understanding of God reaches beyond classical theism, opening to the doctrine of the Supreme Identity or the absolute, unrivalled and utter unity of God.[98] Such a depth of understanding, reflected in numerous Qur'ānic statements, was developed theoretically by the Islamic intellectual and spiritual tradition in the metaphysical articulation of the doctrine of *tawḥīd*, or the unity of God, and realized existentially in the conjoined spiritual states of *fanā'* (passing away) and *baqā'* (subsistence).[99]

2.B.5 Correlation with Modern Science?

There has been considerable effort on the part of Muslims, particularly since Maurice Bucaille's *The Bible, The Qur'ān and Science*,[100] to read the Qur'ān as having anticipated modern scientific findings. While Bucaille's aims in this regard have been rather modest,[101] those of Muslims following in his wake have been less so. Given the prestige of science in the modern era, the desire to associate the Qur'ān with scientific findings in various fields is of course quite understandable. There are, however, several issues to be firmly borne in mind. First, scientific understanding, as a consideration of the history of science readily demonstrates, is itself changeable and thus provides no firm anchor of comparison. Second, the Qur'ān is not—nor by any appearance was meant to be—a scientific text, but rather a reminder to a forgetful and straying humanity and, in this context, a book of "signs" (*āyāt*). Third, many of the physical and cosmological allusions of the Qur'ān, such as the seven heavens, may be better understood under the rubric of traditional symbolism than of modern science. Fourth, what evidence as may be possibly educed from the Qur'ān as being scientific in character is at once brief and allusive, such that associations with scientific findings are typically tenuous at best.

One of the more interesting and suggestive examples, which will serve as a case in point, is that of the multiple allusive parallels in the Qur'ān to the modern scientific understanding of human embryology. The topic was treated by Bucaille as well as by the Canadian embryologist Keith L. Moore.[102] More recently, this analysis has been taken up by Hamza Andreas Tzortzis,[103] who has subsequently distanced himself from such a straightforward "scientific miracles" reading of the Qur'ān to one more nuanced and multivalent.[104] The parallels to the Qur'ān in the case of human embryology remain both intriguing and suggestive, without thereby escaping a certain tenuousness and reasonable doubt. In such a case, a middle way, neither uncritically accepting nor dogmatically denying the possibility of such parallels, would seem most justified. To conclude, the Qur'ān may, in certain instances, point to legitimate parallels with modern scientific findings, without such parallels being subject to firm and secure assertion, given the nature of the Qur'ānic text itself.

3

The Qur'ān and the Messenger

3 · A The Distinctiveness of the Qur'ān

3. A. 1 Distinctiveness of Voice

The Qur'ānic "voice" is readily recognized as distinctive, most immediately from that of the Prophet himself, a distinctiveness of voice consistently maintained over the twenty-three year course of his prophetic career. For those familiar with both the Qur'ān and Hadith literature in classical Arabic, there is no confusing the voice of the Qur'ān from that of the Prophet, the two being readily distinguished, nor does one find these distinctive voices intermingled in the Qur'ān and Hadith literature. For that matter, the voice of the Qur'ān is distinctive from that of other Arabic works generally. Mohammad Khalifa, in giving voice to general opinion, has stated:

> It is distinguished clearly from all other Arabic works whether they be poetry, rhythmic or non-rhythmic prose, the spoken or written language of ordinary people or even that of the Prophet himself.[105]

A. J. Arberry has similarly noted, with specific reference to Muhammad:

> We know quite well how Mohammed spoke in his normal, everyday moods; for his *obiter dicta* have been preserved in

great abundance. It is simply untrue therefore to say, as Margoliouth said, that "it would be difficult to find another case in which there is such a complete identity between the literary work and the mind of the man who produced it." Accepting, as we have good reason to accept, the sayings of Mohammed recorded in the books of Traditions as substantially authentic, and supposing, as Margoliouth supposed, that the Koran was Mohammed's conscious production, it would be more reasonable to say that it would be difficult to find another case in which the literary expression of a man differed so fundamentally from his ordinary speech.[106]

3. A. 2   Stylometric Analysis

The matter of the distinction between the Prophetic and Qur'ānic voices may be investigated with greater analytical rigor through the application of stylometry—the statistical study of linguistic style—most often used in author determination or in discrimination between authors. Such analysis supports the traditional Islamic view that the Qur'ān is at once distinct in authorship from the Prophet and is the work of a single author. The first finding works to undermine any claim that Muhammad is the author of the book; the second finding works to undermine the claim that the book is a collection of borrowings from other sources, such as precedent Jewish or Christian scriptures.

Halim Sayoud has carried out a stylometric analysis in comparison between the Qur'ān and the most canonical collection of Prophetic statements, *Ṣaḥīḥ al-Bukhārī*, and has summarized his work as follows:

> Author discrimination consists of checking whether two texts are written by the same author or not. In this investigation, we try to make an author discrimination between the Qur'ān (the holy words and statements of God in the Islamic religion) and the *Ḥadīth* (statements said by the prophet Muhammad). The Qur'ān is taken in its entirety, whereas for

the Prophet's statements, we chose only the certified texts of the Bukhārī book. Thus, three series of experiments are done and commented on. The first series of experiments analyses the two books in a global form (the text of every book is analyzed as a unique big text). It concerns nine different experiments. The second series of experiments analyses the two books in a segmental form (four different segments of text are extracted from every book). It concerns five different experiments. The third series of experiments makes an automatic authorship attribution of the two books in a segmental form by employing several classifiers and several types of features. The sizes of the segments are more or less in the same range (four different text segments, with approximately the same size, are extracted from every book). It concerns two different experiments. This investigation sheds light on an old enigma, which has not been solved for 14 centuries: in fact, all the results of this investigation have shown that the two books should have two different authors.[107]

In the discussion of the results of his research, he has concluded:

Results of all experiments have led to two main conclusions: (1) First, the two investigated books should have different authors; (2) Second, all the segments that are extracted from a unique book appear to have a certain stylistic similarity. Consequently, we can conclude, according to this investigation, that the Qur'ān was not written by the Prophet Muhammad and that it belongs to a unique author too.[108]

In a more recent extension of this same general study, Sayoud has included a number of additional findings, one of the more notable being the remarkable distinction of vocabularies employed in the two texts:

... we look for the words that are present in one book and absent in the other.... In this experiment, we analyze all the words present in the Ḥadīth, and try to see if there is any occurrence in the Qur'ān. Similarly, on the other hand, we analyze all the words present in the Qur'ān, and try to see if there is any occurrence in the *Ḥadīth*. If a word is present in only one book, it will be retained; otherwise it will not be taken into consideration. The word can be a name, verb, complement or a simple expression.... Results of this experiment show that 62% of the Bukhārī *Ḥadīth* words are untraceable in the Qur'ān and 83% of the Qur'ān words are untraceable in the Bukhārī *Ḥadīth*.... Practically, it is impossible for a same author to write two books (related to a similar topic) with a so great difference in the vocabulary. Therefore, we can deduce that the two books should come from two authors who are characterized by two different vocabularies.[109]

Another stylometric study, carried out by Benham Sadeghi, has focused on the question of whether the Qur'ān has a unique author or, alternatively, bears evidence of being the work of multiple hands. In summarizing his findings, he has concluded:

Literary sources and manuscript evidence indicate that the Prophet Muhammad disseminated the contents of the Qur'ān, and that the Caliph 'Uthmān dispatched master copies of the scripture to several cities. As a thought experiment, however, let us unlearn what we know, imagining that we had come across the Qur'ān not knowing where it came from or who disseminated it. In fact, let us even overlook the semantic contents of the text. What could one conclude about the Qur'ān's composition just from the formal-stylistic patterns observed? One would conclude that *style backs the hypothesis of one author*.... The study reveals the stylistic continuity and distinctiveness of the text as a whole. As far as this point is concerned, the present study makes palpable what we knew already: no competent and seasoned scholar of the Qur'ān, while aware of the stylistic variation in the text, could lose sight of its underlying unity.[110]

3. A. 3 Distinctiveness of Personality

Not only is the Qur'ānic voice distinct from that of Muhammad, but so also is the "personality" reflected in the Qur'ān. Far from being the central figure of the Qur'ān, he is in fact largely marginal to it, far less prominent than other figures such as Abraham, Moses, Jesus and Mary. Further, events of profound concern in the Prophet's life, such as the death of his wife Khadījah or the loss of his children, are rarely, if ever, addressed. Further yet, the Qur'ān on occasion dominates over the Prophet, offering sharp correction to his behavior or course of action, as when he turned away, while attempting to win one of the Meccan nobles to his cause, from a blind man asking for religious instruction.[111] As M. A. Draz has observed:

> It is not true that the Qur'ān reflects the personality of the Prophet. Far from it. Most of the time it passes him by in silence, and treats him as a total abstraction. When it does mention him, it does so to judge, direct or dominate him. His joys and daily sufferings—the deep grief he felt at the death of his children or friends, the Year of Mourning in which he lost his wife and uncle and with them all the moral support which had sustained him during his preaching campaign—do we see the slightest echo of these in the Qur'ān? But as soon as his life is concerned with a matter of moral conduct, we see him in the grips of its legislative authority, as a subjected soul, the one often opposing itself to the other as intransigence versus clemency, extreme frankness versus timidity, patience versus impatience. And it is not rare for Qur'ānic teachings to contain severe reproaches for the slightest deviation on the part of the Prophet in relation to the ideal proposed.[112]

Additionally, Qur'ānic guidance was in no way guaranteed to the Prophet at his convenience, as with the long delay of Qur'ānic vindication with regard to the scandal surrounding his young wife 'Ā'isha.[113] As Martin Lings has narrated:

But the delay of this Revelation, although painful to the Prophet and his followers, was in reality an added strength. His worst enemies refused to draw conclusions from it, but for those Quraysh who were in two minds it was a powerful corroboration of his claim that the Revelation came to him from Heaven and that he had no part in it and no control over it. Was it conceivable that if Muhammad had invented the earlier Revelations he could have delayed so long before inventing this latest one, especially when so much appeared to be at stake?[114]

3. A. 4 Distinctiveness of Past Knowledge

Although the Qur'ān is not particularly concerned with the revealing of past knowledge or prophesying of future knowledge, there are a handful of instances of both that may be identified. With regard to the former category, an example that may be mentioned involves, in distinction to the Old Testament, the proper temporal usage of the word "Pharaoh". In the conclusion of their study of the topic, M. S. M. Saifullah, 'Abdullah David and Elias Karim have observed:

> According to modern linguistic research the word "Pharaoh" comes from the Egyptian *per-aa*, meaning the "Great House" and originally referred to the palace rather than the king himself. The word was used by the writers of the Old Testament and has since become a widely adopted title for all the kings of Egypt. However, the Egyptians did not call their ruler "Pharaoh" until the 18th Dynasty (*c*.1552–1295 BC) in the New Kingdom Period. In the language of the hieroglyphs, "Pharaoh" was first used to refer to the king during the reign of Amenophis IV (*c*.1352–1338 BC). We know that such a designation was correct in the time of Moses but the use of the word Pharaoh in the story of Joseph is an anachronism, as under the rule of the Hyksos there was no "Pharaoh".... With regard to the Egyptian king who was

a contemporary of Joseph, the Qur'ān uses the title "King" (Arabic, *Malik*); he is never once addressed as Pharaoh. As for the king who ruled during the time of Moses, the Qur'ān repeatedly calls him Pharaoh (Arabic, *Fir'awn*). These facts that we have mentioned were unknown at the time of the Qur'ānic Revelation.[115]

Another example that may be mentioned involves the Qur'ānic description of the fate of an ancient South Arabian society, one subsequently corroborated archeologically. As Toby Mayer has argued:

> In regard to this, the last chapter of the volume (XXI) yet again turns to the prospect of archaeological corroboration from South Arabia for data in the Qur'ān. The issue here concerns Qur'ān 34: 15–16 and the extraordinary reference there to the fate of the society of Sabā, in Yemen. Rippin is unable to sidestep the conclusion that genuinely ancient information in the Qur'ān is found at this point. The information has been generally viewed as relating in particular to Mārib, a society which depended on the maintenance of a sophisticated dam-system. When the dam gave way, the people of Mārib met their fate, and the rich landscape returned to desert. At this point in the Qur'ān we find a *hapax legomenon* [a word only appearing on a single occasion], the mysterious term *'arim*—with the relevant expression, *sayl al-'arim*, generally being rendered into English as "the flood of the dam". This expression is not familiar in Arabic and is inescapably a loan-word from epigraphical South Arabian. It turns out that the word is actually cognate with Akkadian *arimmu*, meaning a dam. Excitingly, inscriptions at Mārib dating from circa 450 and 540 CE refer to the dam using this very word, *'ayn-rā'-mīm*.[116]

3. A. 5 Distinctiveness of Future Knowledge

With regard to the latter category of future knowledge, an example that may be mentioned involves a pair of unrelated, roughly concurrent military victories. As Hamza Mustafa Njozi has commented:

> The fact that the Qur'ān had made definite statements about future events, and all of which came to pass, weakens the idea that the Qur'ān is the product of Muhammad's experience. To cite but just two examples, the Qur'ān in chapter 30 verses 1–7 (which were revealed in 615 AD) clearly states that even though the Roman Empire has been defeated by the Persians, they will nevertheless, within a few years, be victorious. The Arabic word used to describe "a few years" is *biḍ'i*, which means between 3 to 9 years. And this is precisely what happened. Seven years after the prophecy the Romans defeated the Persians. What is equally stunning, the prophecy says, *"On that day the believers would also be victorious,"* and simultaneously the Muslims were celebrating over the Quraysh in the Battle of Badr, as Hingora says: "Accordingly, this prophecy was exactly fulfilled when Heraclius defeated the Persians at the decisive battle of Issus in 622 CE and the Romans victoriously entered the heart of Persia in 624 CE. Exactly in the same year the Muslims gained victory over the Meccan Pagans at Badr and the believers 'rejoiced on that day' as prophesied in the Qur'ān."[117]

Another example that may be mentioned involves the eventual fate of the body of the Pharaoh who was drowned pursuing the Israelites. Maurice Bucaille has noted that, in contrast to the account in Exodus, the Qur'ānic narrative of the drowning of Pharaoh additionally predicted the future preservation of his body, a preservation that later 19th century archaeology was to confirm:

> "And We took the Children of Israel across the sea, and Pharaoh and his soldiers pursued them in tyranny and enmity until, when drowning overtook him, he said, 'I believe that there is no deity except that in whom the Children of Israel believe, and I am of the Muslims'—Now? And you had disobeyed [Him] before and were of the corrupters?—So

today We will save you in body that you may be to those who succeed you a sign. And indeed, many among the people, of Our signs, are heedless" [Qur'ān 10: 90–92]. This is all that the *sūrah* contains on the Pharaoh's death.... The text of the Qur'ān merely states very clearly that the Pharaoh's body will be saved: that is the important piece of information. When the Qur'ān was transmitted to man by the Prophet, the bodies of all the Pharaohs who are today considered (rightly or wrongly) to have something to do with the Exodus were in their tombs of the Necropolis of Thebes, on the opposite side of the Nile from Luxor. At the time however, absolutely nothing was known of this fact, and it was not until the end of the nineteenth century that they were discovered there. As the Qur'ān states, the body of the Pharaoh of the Exodus was in fact rescued: whichever of the Pharaohs it was, visitors may see him in the Royal Mummies Room of the Egyptian Museum, Cairo.[118]

3 · b The Position of the Messenger

3.b.1 Prophetic Character

A consideration with which the standard polemical claim of Muhammad as author of the Qur'ān must contend is his consistently reported character, particularly his trustworthiness, as witnessed both prior to and during his ostensible prophetic career. Such an observation points to the inherent implausibility of the polemical claim of Muhammad's authorship. The character, integrity and sincerity of the Prophet may be judged both directly, as reflected in the traditional accounts of his life, as well as indirectly, as reflected in the loyalty, devotion and conduct inspired in those who followed him and who knew him intimately. As Mohammad Khalifa has noted:

> Had Muhammad not been sincere in his prophethood and honest in delivering his revelations his friends and followers

59

would never have been so devoted to him, nor would they have clung to his teachings despite devastating hardship and persecution. It is a remarkable tribute to the character of Muhammad and to those of his friends and followers that not one of them ever betrayed him.[119]

W. Montgomery Watt has similarly weighed:

Since Carlyle's lecture on Muhammad in *Heroes and Hero-Worship*, the West has been aware that there was a good case to be made out for believing in Muhammad's sincerity. His readiness to undergo persecutions for his beliefs, the high moral character of the men who believed in him and looked up to him as leader, and the greatness of his ultimate achievement—all argue his fundamental integrity. To suppose Muhammad an impostor raises more problems than it solves. Moreover, none of the great figures of history is so poorly appreciated in the West as Muhammad.[120]

3. B. 2   Lack of Prophetic Motivation

The polemical claim of the Qur'ān as deliberately authored by Muhammad ignores the fact that for the first dozen years of his prophetic career, prior to the Hijra, or emigration to Medina, his prophetic activities put him in progressively difficult and dangerous circumstances, leading to his ostracization, impoverishment, the death of his beloved wife and his own near assassination. The emigration itself was at once an exile from his home and an immensely uncertain gamble, one involving repeated threats to his life in the context of skirmishing and warfare. If Muhammad was the author of the Qur'ān, his preaching of it was profoundly against his own personal interests, fundamentally destroying his standing in his community—in which he had been both wealthy and well respected—in the context of an overriding tribalism in which such a course could be quite literally suicidal.

The orientation of Muhammad with respect to wealth and

luxury when such were well within his grasp is yet another indication of his lack of worldly motivation. Embracing a voluntary poverty and simplicity of life, he was not only for the poor, in terms of social welfare and charity, but of the poor as well. As his young wife 'Ā'isha recalled: "A complete month would pass by during which we would not make a fire (for cooking), and our food used to be only dates and water unless we were given a present of some meat."[121] Similarly, as Martin Lings has narrated:

> The Prophet and his family had lived a life of utmost frugality. 'Ā'isha said that before [the battle of] Khaybar she had not known what it was to eat her fill of dates. Such was the poverty of their ever-increasing dependents that the Prophet's wives had only asked him for what they needed, and not always that. Things that could be dispensed with were given away, or else sold so that the money could be charitably spent.[122]

It might be argued that, even if Muhammad lacked personal motives for authoring the Qur'ān, he may have done so out of a high-minded desire for the moral betterment of his people. Hamza Mustafa Njozi has noted the contradiction of lofty goal and low method that such a theory imposes:

> In view of the above difficulties, some scholars have put forward moral reformation as a probable motive which actuated Muhammad to compose the Qur'ān. The reformation theory presents several problems. Moral reformation is a noble objective which could be achieved without resorting to immoral acts like deceit and lies. The reason for his choice of immoral means to build a moral society is neither clear nor stated by the proponents of this theory.[123]

3. B. 3 Lack of Prophetic Capability

Another consideration with which the standard polemical claim of Muhammad as author of the Qur'ān must contend is his lack of learning and of poetic gifts, to which might

61

be added the lack of an *in situ* Arab tradition of revealed wisdom or prophecy from which he might draw. The lack of learning—particularly his "unletteredness"—is emphasized in the tradition, but his lack of poetic gifts is also of particular relevance: the Arabs had great poets and were highly sensitive to the poetic possibilities of the Arabic language—Muhammad simply did not display such gifts, apart from the Qur'ān itself, either prior to or during his prophetic career. Ernest McClain has expressed the fundamental issue quite pointedly:

> "This is a Message sent down from the Lord of the Worlds" to an honored apostle; "it is not the word of a poet" (LXIX 41 and 43). If it seems awkward for us to accept this denial of Muhammad's authorship, it proves even more awkward in the end, when we comprehend the Qur'ān more fully, to explain how an essentially uneducated merchant-trader in 7th century Arabia could possibly have produced such a document.[124]

As Navid Kermani has further commented:

> He had not studied the difficult craft of poetry, when he started reciting verses publicly... Yet Muhammad's recitations differed from poetry and from the rhyming prose of the soothsayers, the other conventional form of inspired, metrical speech at the time.[125]

Muḥammad Taqī 'Usmānī has similarly observed:

> Such a proclamation was no ordinary thing. It came from a person who had never learned anything from the renowned poets and scholars of the time, had never recited even a single piece of poetry in their poetic congregations, had never attended the company of soothsayers. And far from composing any poetry himself, he did not even remember the verses of other poets.[126]

Finally, as M. A. S. Abdel Haleem has cogently argued:

> Our colleagues in Oriental departments might say that it

is Muhammad who wrote the Qur'ān or even others. The theological tradition, on the other hand, maintains that he received it from an archangel who delivered it to him from God. But, as a scholar of linguistics, I deal with this only from the linguistic point of view. And I can see that what Muhammad received in the "state of revelation" was very different from his normal language. We can see, for example, that the Qur'ān is clearly of a higher level than the language of the *Ḥadīth* (reports of the sayings and actions of the Prophet). We also know what Muhammad was capable of. We know that until his forties [when the Qur'ān was first communicated] he didn't write any poetry and that he never gave speeches in public. It makes one wonder therefore how he, all of the sudden, could start to recite these verses of the Qur'ān. The Muslims of the time said that the language came from God. The non-Muslims, however, said that he was a poet or that he had a jinn who told him to say all the things he said. But whatever their explanation, they agreed on one thing: that the style of the Qur'ān was much higher than the language people were used to. I have read the Qur'ān for such a long time and I know it by heart but still, every day when I read the Qur'ān, I discover new meanings in certain verses which I hadn't seen before. That's a special quality of the language of the Qur'ān—even apart from the faith.[127]

3. B. 4 Possibility of External Instruction

A polemical claim sometimes made is that Muhammad was instructed by another person, one well-versed in earlier Jewish or Christian scriptures, in his ostensible crafting or deliverance of his message. Such an argument founders on two principal difficulties. First, it only pushes the problem of the source of the Qur'ān's inspired and inspiring character back one level and leaves the fundamental question of its origins unresolved. Second, it ignores the close proximity in which Muhammad lived with his family, companions and followers and the extreme difficulty that such proximity would impose on any such proposed collaboration, particularly over an extended period. The Qur'ān itself addresses one such accusation raised by Muhammad's adversaries, as Jamal Badawi has noted:

> The Qur'ān puts it very nicely and shows an important logical flaw for this accusation which appears in *sūrah* (16: 103): "We know indeed that they say, 'It is a man that teaches him.' The tongue of him they wickedly point to is notably foreign, while this is Arabic, pure and clear." This fellow actually only knew broken Arabic, so how could a person with that foreign tongue with broken Arabic be the teacher of the Prophet in producing a Book which challenged the most eloquent of the eloquent to produce something similar to it? It is similar to saying that a Chinese immigrant in Britain was the one who taught Shakespeare. This just doesn't make any sense at all. These are examples of people who were known not to be pagan but there were obviously no grounds to relate that the source of the Qur'ān was from them.[128]

Touching upon the second difficulty raised, Badawi has further noted:

> There are additional reasons, as the life of the Prophet was open to all. The Qur'ān testifies to that fact in *sūrah* 49 and that he did not even have sufficient privacy in his own home because people were around him at all times and were trying to record each and every word that he said. They tried to observe his action as a model for them. As this was the case, how could it be that he was secretly meeting with a teacher while people were around him and in his presence at all times? How could he have escaped the open eyes that were around him all the time, including those of men who were independent and had strong personalities like Abū Bakr and 'Uthmān?[129]

4

The Qur'ān and its Auditors

4 · A   Positive Judgments upon the Qur'ān

4. A. 1   Excellence of Language (Arabic)

The literary excellence of the Arabic Qur'ān has, since its earliest inception, been one of its most compelling features. It is also one of the Qur'ān's own internal claims for its authenticity: "And if you are in doubt concerning that We have sent down on Our servant, then bring a *sūrah* like it, and call your witnesses, apart from God, if you are truthful." [Qur'ān 2: 23] Throughout Islamic history, the Qur'ān has remained a literary touchstone of excellence in Arabic letters, without rival or peer either in comparison to what went before it or what was to come after. As Martin Zammit has judged:

> Notwithstanding the literary excellence of some of the long pre-Islamic poems... the Qur'ān is definitely on a level of its own as the most eminent written manifestation of the Arabic language.[130]

Jane D. McAuliffe has similarly observed:

> For those who do speak Arabic, the aural and textual beauty of the Qur'ān has been avowed for centuries. The sheer majesty of the language, its rhetorical force and the vitality of its rhythmical cadences produce a powerful impact on people who can appreciate its linguistic and literary qualities.[131]

Touching upon the key Qur'ānic notion of the inimitability of the text, Kristina Nelson has noted:

> The beauty of the Qur'ānic language and style is itself considered a proof of the divine origin of the text. This idea, expressed in the concept of *i'jāz* (inimitability), thus adds an aesthetic dimension to the Qur'ān—not only is it an expression of the nature of the divine, and of the human in relation to the divine, it is a model of beauty to which human expression can only aspire. In that regard, the language of the Qur'ān has served for 1,400 years as the exalted standard for Classical Literary Arabic in matters of syntax, vocabulary, rhetoric, and, to a large extent, phonetics.[132]

The aesthetic impact of the Qur'ān is central to its peculiarly compelling character. Such has been its effect that Islamic history is replete with accounts of individuals converted on the spot after having heard the Qur'ān recited.[133] As Nasr Abu Zayd has recounted:

> The Qur'ānic language, though human as it is, has captured the imagination of the Arabs from the very moment of its revelation due to the linguistic transformation of meaning into semiotics. The reports about the influence of the Qur'ān's recitation over individuals are abundant. Many stories are preserved in Islamic literature according to which even the unbelievers were fascinated by the overwhelming poetic effect of the Qur'ānic language, an effect incomparable to that of poetry.[134]

Neither has the inimitable beauty of the text been lost, in the main and in the end, on Western scholars, as Shabbir Akhtar has noted:

> It is the unanimous verdict of critical, including hostile, Arabist opinion, that the Qur'ān has been for fourteen centuries the crowning achievement of a rich and varied Arabic literature. Even disbelieving Arabists eventually concede that the Qur'ān's Arabic is outstandingly stylish: most of them reverse,

after a whole lifetime of study and reflection, their own earlier dismissive judgments made in the active heat of juvenile "scholarship" and missionary zeal. All competent authorities agree that while a translation could successfully convey the sense and the learned nuances of its fecund and mysterious vocabulary, it can never register the sheer range of its emotional effect. The unsettling impact of the recited scripture's sustained eloquence even on disbelievers is noted by western scholars who espouse a phenomenological approach to religion.[135]

4. A. 2 Linguistic Richness

A key aspect of the literary excellence of the Qur'ān is the sheer richness of its use with respect to the possibilities of the Arabic language. As Kasim Randeree has masterfully summarized:

The Qur'ān is thus an independent genre in its own right, comprising of two inseparable elements; rhetorical and cohesive elements. Rhetoric can be defined as the use of language to please or persuade, *"the conveying of meaning in the best of verbal forms."* Cohesiveness is the feature that binds sentences to each other grammatically and lexically. It also refers to how words are linked together into sentences and how sentences are in turn linked together to form larger units in texts. These rhetorical and cohesive components of the Qur'ānic text cannot be divorced from each other. The Qur'ān utilizes numerous rhetorical features including, but not limited to, rhythm, figures of speech, similes, metaphors, rhetorical questions, the use of irony and the repetition of words.

Its cohesiveness includes various methods such as parallelistic structures, phrasal ties, substitution, reference and lexical cohesion. These features provide the bedrock and hang together to create the Qur'ān's unique genre. In contrast, non-Qur'ānic Arabic texts mostly employ cohesive elements but the Qur'ān uses both cohesive and rhetorical elements in every verse. Furthermore, in contrast to the non-Qur'ānic structure, this arrangement provides a pleasing, sweet acoustic effect, called euphony, which itself is a rhetorical feature.

The frequency of rhetorical features in the Qur'ān is unparalleled, surpassing any other Arabic text, classical or modern. These include analogy (88: 15–6, 93: 9–10); alliteration (33: 71, 77: 20); antiphrasis (44: 49); antithesis (35: 7, 9: 82); asyndeton (13: 2); assonance (88: 25–6, 88: 14–5); cadence (present in the whole Qur'ān); chiasmus (3: 27); epizeuxis (94: 5–6); equivoque (24: 43); homonymy (2: 14–5, 3: 54); hyperbole (7: 40, 33: 10, 39: 71–2); isocolon (65: 7–10); metaphor (19: 4, 21: 18); metonymy (54: 13, 6: 127); parenthesis (7: 42, 4: 73); polyptoton (80: 25–26); rhetorical questions (55: 60, 37: 91–2); stress (29: 62, 3: 92); and synecdoche (90: 12–3).

According to one analysis, just over 50% of the whole Qur'ān ends with the same letter. This particular use of rhyme, in a text the size of the Qur'ān, has not been replicated in any Arabic text. However the Qur'ān does not conform to a constant or consistent rhyme, which reflects the work of Al-Rummani, who states that the Qur'ān's use of language is semantically orientated and does not conform to a particular style.

Furthermore, the Qur'ān is awash with stylistic variation. Stylistic variation is the use of different features of language in a multitude of ways and is a branch of linguistics which studies the features of the varieties of language within a given situation, context and meaning. Stylistics also tries to develop principles to explain the particular choices made by the author. Hajjaji-Jarrah discusses how the Qur'ān achieves its uniqueness due to stylistic differences, stating, "... Qur'ānic 'Arabiyya (Arabic) brings forth a dazzling assembly of word meaning and sound defying the conventions of both the Arabian *saj*' and the literary rules of classical Arabic literature."

There are a myriad of ways the Qur'ān uses language which is unknown in any Arabic discourse, some of these include: semantically orientated assonance and rhyme; *iltifāt* or grammatical shifts; interrelation between sound, structure and meaning; unique linguistic genre; and word order.[136]

4. A. 3 Interpenetration and Simultaneity

The Qur'ān is a remarkably homogeneous and consistent text, indeed possessing what might be termed a "holographic" character, in which any given portion of the text often contains most or all of its principal themes. This character, one that tends to run hard against Western assumptions of textual linearity, is at once an interpenetration and a simultaneity, a kind of unity pervading multiplicity that, as it were, recapitulates the central Qur'ānic doctrine of *tawḥīd*, or Divine unity, in the body of the text itself. As Abdul Wadod Shalabi has observed:

> One of the most surprising features of the Qur'ān to the Western reader coming to it for the first time is the way in which subjects of many kinds may be found together in a single chapter, or even in the course of a few verses. This is an essential aspect of the Book's message. It is human nature to endeavor to categorize and label our experience of the world, and we feel disconcerted when our familiar expectations of such an ordering are not fulfilled. The Qur'ān, both in its literary style and in its internal arrangement, conforms to no human norms. It is a message which has broken through the veil of the unseen and causes us to look upwards, bringing us suddenly into a new dimension, a new mode of perception. The Qur'ān is from the One, and it belongs to a higher order of creation than our own, where unity and differentiation begin to coalesce, and where our perception of a world dispersed into multiple states and forms loses its validity. But despite this unique feature, the formal message, the outward meaning of the Book, is in no way compromised; indeed, it gains in cogency, for each of its teachings and guiding principles is meaningful only in the context of the transcendent unity of God.[137]

Kristina Nelson has similarly captured the sense of the Qur'ānic text as breaking through time and historicity, as opening a window to the transcendent and the eternal:

> The surface logic of the content of the Qur'ān is not readily apparent at first reading. The themes and subject matter are not systematically developed; rather, aspects, repetitions, or varied images of the same theme are woven throughout the whole. The effect, on superficial reading, is one of abrupt and bewildering shifts in subject, mood, and speaker, of "human language crushed by the power of the Divine Word... human language... scattered into a thousand fragments like a wave scattered into drops against the rocks at sea."[138]

> Some Muslim scholars attempt to explain the underlying unity of the text, but the clue to the perception of that unity lies in the Muslim's participation in a society founded on revelation. Islamic revelation abolishes the atomism of tense: there is no past, no present, no future, but one absolute present. The revelation is the past in that it is the beginning and source of knowledge and action. It is the present in its continuousness, and the future in that it is the complete and final message. The moment of revelation is eternal. This transcendence of linear time is manifested in various ways in the text. There is no systematic treatment of the material, whether it be law or history. For example, a single narrative may be episodically scattered throughout the text (the story of Joseph, sura 12, is an exception), and not necessarily in chronological order. The story of Moses, for example, can be traced as follows: Moses' childhood (20: 38–40, 28: 7–13); Moses called by God (19: 51–3, 2: 9–56, 28: 29–35); Moses and Pharaoh (7: 103–137, 10: 75–92, 11: 96–9), and so forth. Moreover, each part of the text refers to other parts, by means of association and repetition of image, phrase, and rhythm, so that the whole is constantly present.[139]

Finally, Norman O. Brown, bringing in a series of remarkable parallels, has educed:

Massignon speaks of transhistorical, or meta-historical, tele-scoping; systematic anachronism. Islam is committed by the Koran to project a metahistorical plane on which the eter-nal meaning of historical events is disclosed. It is that plane on which Moses and Elijah are seen conversing with Jesus in Matthew 17; that plane on which Dante's *Divine Comedy* unfolds; and Blake's prophetic books; and *Finnegans Wake*. History *sub specie aeternitatis*.

There is an apocalyptic or eschatological style: every surah is an epiphany and a portent; a warning, "plain tokens that haply we may take heed" (24: 1). The apocalyptic style is *totum simul*, simultaneous totality: the whole in every part. Marshall Hodgson, in *The Venture of Islam*—still the outstanding and only ecumenical Western history—says of the Koran, "Almost every element which goes to make up its message is somehow present in any given passage." Simultaneous totality, as in *Finnegans Wake*. Or, more generally, what Umberto Eco calls "The Poetics of the Open Work": "We can see it as an infinite contained within finiteness. The work therefore has infinite aspects, because each of them, and any moment of it, contains the totality of the work." Eco is trying to characterize a revolution in the aesthetic sensibility of the West: we are the first generation in the West able to read the Koran, if we are able to read *Finnegans Wake*. In fact Carlyle's reaction to the Koran—"a wearisome confused jumble, crude, incondite; endless iterations, long-windedness, entanglement"—is exactly our first reaction to *Finnegans Wake*. The affinity between this most recalcitrant of sacred texts and this most avant-garde of literary experiments is a sign of our times. Joyce was fully aware of the connection, as Atherton shows in the most exciting chapter of *The Books at the Wake*; I particularly like his discovery in the *Wake* of the titles of 111 of the 114 surahs.

... Hence, it does not matter in what order you read the Koran: it is all there all the time; and it is supposed to be all there all the time in your mind or at the back of your mind, memorized and available for appropriate quotation and collage into your conversation or your writing, or your action.... Every surah is an epiphany and a portent; and therefore not beautiful but sublime.[140]

4. A. 4 Persuasion and Argument

It might reasonably be said that the first task of the Qur'ān's discourse with respect to its earliest audience was precisely that of persuasion regarding its claims of authenticity. Certainly, this persuasion was in part grounded in its own literary impact, but it was also just as significantly grounded in the argument and rhetoric it brought to bear. Had the Qur'ān not succeeded in this task, both among its earliest audience as well as subsequent generations, no one presently would be much exercised with respect to it. In the context of such discourse, the Qur'ān presents its own arguments for the acceptance of its general authenticity and specific truth claims, engaging in numerous rhetorical strategies of persuasion. Although such strategies have been touched upon elsewhere,[141] a comprehensive treatment may be found in Rosalind Ward Gwynne's *Logic, Rhetoric and Legal Reasoning in the Qur'ān*.[142] As she has observed in her introduction:

> I believe that the reader will be surprised at how thick with argument the Qur'ān actually is. It has long been common practice to analyze the Qur'ān's historical and legal material, Biblical parallels and divergences, punishment-stories, rhetorical figures, vocabulary and grammar, data that bear on the life of the Prophet and other thematic selections— all indispensable disciplines. But after having previously concentrated upon some of the areas mentioned above, I found that analyzing Qur'ānic argument was like discovering a trove of hidden verses.[143]

In outlining the various persuasive strategies and techniques deployed by the Qur'ān, which include such instances as "ten of the nineteen possible moods of the Aristotelian categorical syllogism"[144] and "conditional and disjunctive syllogisms as originally schematized by logicians of the Stoic school,"[145] Gwynne has explicitly listed as follows:

> The text of the Qur'ān, closely examined, yields more than thirty varieties of explicit and implicit argument, elements of argument, techniques, and demonstrations.

> Here is a schematic outline of the arguments that appear in this book:

> 1) The Covenant.

> 2) Signs and precedents.

> 3) The *Sunna* of God.

> 4) Rules, commands, and reasons why: Does God work for a purpose?; Rule-based reasoning; The logic of commands; Commands, commandments and purpose.

> 5) Legal arguments: Reciprocity and recompense; Priority, equivalence, entailment, and limitation; Distinction and exception; Aristotle's "Non-Artistic" proofs: laws, witnesses, contracts, torture, and oaths; An excursus on performatives.

> 6) Comparison: Similarity; Analogy; Parable; Degree.

> 7) Contrast: Difference; Inequality; Opposition; Opposites and contraries; Contradictories; Reversal; Antithesis.

> 8) Categorical arguments.

> 9) Conditional and disjunctive arguments.

> 10) Technical terms and debating technique.[146]

Finally, in her conclusion, Gwynne has quite tellingly noted: "Reasoning and argument are so integral to the content of the Qur'ān and so inseparable from its structure that they in many ways shaped the very consciousness of Qur'ānic scholars."[147]

4. A. 5 Experience of Presence

Quite apart from its surface meaning, and even its impact of language, the Qur'ān also seems to possess a mysterious "presence" experienced through the facade of the text. As Seyyed Hossein Nasr has noted:

> The Qur'ān contains a quality which is difficult to express in modern language. One might call it a divine magic, if one understands it metaphysically and not literally. The formulae of the Qur'ān, because they come from God, have a power which is not identical with what we learn from them rationally by simply reading and reciting them. They are rather a talisman which protects and guides man. That is why even the physical presence of the Qur'ān carries a great grace or *barakah* with it.[148]

Similarly, as T. J. Winter has commented:

> When we read the Qur'ān... we also recognize that it is to do with seeing that the text is not exhausted by its outward horizon and that it has depths. And one of the experiences that believers most frequently have is, as it were, falling into the text... a moment of sudden opening and there seems to be a crack in the page and we fall into the book. And many of the *'ulamā'* [scholars] who have reflected on the subtleties of the book—like Shāh Walī Allah Dihlawī, for instance—have commented on this.[149]

Fred M. Denny has, in similar regard, remarked:

> While writing my doctoral dissertation, I lived for many months in an intimate, daily relationship with the Arabic Qur'ān and its exegetical tradition. I was gratified that, contrary to what some Western critics of Islam might have anticipated, I never became bored with the Qur'ān, nor was made impatient by its occasional repetitiveness, but felt drawn ever more deeply into its unique, mysterious world of meaning, expression, and feeling. Sometimes, when comparing passages

on selected themes over the chronological periods of its revelation, I received insights that included an apperception that
the Qur'ān was reading me as much as I was reading it. That
realization did not frighten or "spook" me; rather it inspired
me and engendered trust in the text's goodness and power.
I wondered if this experience was a prelude to conversion or
simply awareness of divine hospitality to a guest who has been
honored with a share in its open secret of revelation.[150]

As the previous account suggests, the peculiar power of the
Arabic Qur'ān is by no means limited to Muslims, as Michael
Sells has narrated:

One afternoon in Cairo, I found myself in an unusual
situation. The streets of this noisy, bustling city were suddenly
strangely quiet, yet the cafes were crowded with people
clustered around televisions. For special events—the death of
a great figure, an important soccer game—one might expect
to find people in cafes following the event on television. What
had drawn people from the streets into the cafes today was the
appearance of one of Egypt's popular Qur'ān reciters. When
I returned to my hotel, the lobby was filled with men, some
of them Egyptian Christians, watching and listening to the
televised recitation with intense interest.

Such appreciation for the recited Qur'ān stimulates a diver-
sity of explanations. To devout Muslims, the recited Qur'ān
is the word of God revealed to the prophet Muhammad; its
divine origin accounts for its hold over the listener. Some
anti-Islamic missionaries attribute the extraordinary power
and beauty of the Qur'ān to a Jinni or even Satan. A Marxist
revolutionary from an Islamic background, who was highly
critical of all religion, insisted that the genius of the Qur'ān
resulted from Muhammad's alleged madness and resultant
close contact with the unconscious. In Middle Eastern soci-
eties, what unites these opinions and seems beyond dispute is
the fact that the recited Qur'ān is a distinctively compelling
example of verbal expression.[151]

4 · B Negative Judgments upon the Qur'ān

4. B. 1 Question of Quality (in Translation)

If the Arabic Qur'ān has a remarkably compelling attraction, the same cannot be generally said of the Qur'ān in translation. As Karen Armstrong has expressed:

> Western people find the Koran a difficult book and this is largely a problem of translation. Arabic is particularly difficult to translate: even ordinary literature and the mundane utterances of politicians frequently sound stilted and alien when translated into English, for example, and this is doubly true of the Koran, which is written in dense and highly allusive, elliptical speech. The early surahs in particular give the impression of human language crushed and splintered under the divine impact. Muslims often say that when they read the Koran in a translation, they feel that they are reading a different book because nothing of the beauty of the Arabic has been conveyed.[152]

Michael Sells has similarly observed the profound dichotomy of experience between the Qur'ān in Arabic versus in translation:

> Most of the world's Muslims, including the majority of those who live outside the Arab world, learn the Qur'ān in Arabic. For them, the sense of some extraordinary power and beauty in its language is readily recognized. Generations of Qur'ānic commentators have tried to account for the compelling nature of the composition, articulation, or voice of the Qur'ān in Arabic, but the fact that there was something special about it was assumed. It was apparent from the love of people for the Qur'ānic voice; from the intertwining of the Qur'ānic allusions and rhythms in the rich fabric of art, literature, and music; from the way the Qur'ān is recited at great occasions and in the most humble circumstances of daily life; and from the devotion people put into learning to recite it correctly in

Arabic. The sound of Qur'ānic recitation can move people to tears, from 'Umar, the powerful second Caliph of Islam, to the average farmer, villager, or townsman of today, including those who may not be particularly observant or religious in temperament.

Yet for Westerners who do not read or speak Arabic, the effort to get even a basic glimpse of what the Qur'ān is about has proved frustrating. The Qur'ān is not arranged in chronological order or narrative pattern. Indeed, the passages associated with the very first revelations given to Muhammad, those learned first by Muslims when they study the Qur'ān in Arabic, are placed at the very end of the written Qur'ān. After a short prayer, the written Qur'ān begins with the longest and one of the most complex chapters, one from Muhammad's later career, which engages the full array of legal, historical, polemical, and religious issues in a fashion bewildering for the reader not immersed in the history and law of early Islam. For those familiar with the Bible, it would be as if the second page opened with a combination of the legal discussions in Leviticus, the historical polemic in the book of Judges, and apocalyptic allusions from Revelation, with the various topics mixed in together and beginning in mid-topic.[153]

T.J. Winter has further developed this dichotomy in comparison to the more readily grasped experience of music:

The Koran is a profoundly rhetorical document, addressing a culture whose sole major aesthetic form was poetry. The Koran is not itself poetry; it is set in a kind of dynamic prose, with highly complex assonances, rhymes, and internal rhythms. But it is poetic inasmuch as the form of its discourse interacts intimately with the meaning that it conveys. This may be one reason why the various English translations are so unsuccessful as literature: the meaning is inseparable from the splendor of the language. Reading the Koran in English can be like reading the libretto of, say, *Fidelio*, with all the repeats included. Without the music it can seem reiterative and

77

prosaic. To translate the Koran is to strip it of its orchestral accompaniment, which is its splendidly Arabic matrix. This is, in fact, an interesting theological difficulty for Muslims: the faith is claimed to be addressed universally to all nations, and yet its scripture, on whose credibility its claims stand or fall, is not perfectly accessible to the majority of mankind who do not know Arabic.[154]

4. B. 2 Question of Textual Coherence

The apparent incoherence, or lack of structure, in the Qur'ānic text is often a stumbling block for Western readers, serving further as an undermining factor of judgment regarding its claims of Divine authorship. As Frithjof Schuon has observed:

Seen from outside, however, this book appears (apart from approximately the last quarter, the form of which is highly poetic, though it is not poetry) to be a collection of sayings and stories that is more or less incoherent and sometimes incomprehensible at first approach. The reader who is not forewarned, whether he reads the text in translation or in Arabic, runs up against obscurities, repetitions, tautologies and, in most of the long surahs, against a certain dryness, unless he has at least the "sensory consolation" of that beauty of sound which emerges from ritual and correctly intoned reading... The seeming incoherence... always has the same cause, namely the incommensurable disproportion between the Spirit on the one hand and the limited resources of human language on the other: it is as though the poor and coagulated language of mortal man would break under the formidable pressure of the Heavenly Word into a thousand fragments, or as if God, in order to express a thousand truths, had but a dozen words at his disposal and so was compelled to make use of allusions heavy with meaning, of ellipses, abridgements and symbolical syntheses.[155]

What may appear as incoherence may be revealed, upon

deeper consideration, to possess a profound coherence and unity of structure, as M. A. S. Abdel Haleem has noted:

> I am convinced that there is a great unity in the material of every single *sūrah*. People often think it is a jumble of things. But it isn't. Through long studies of the "linguistic habits" of the Qur'ān I can tell you that it is meticulously put together. The particular order of the *sūrahs* is a different story however. Even Muslim scholars themselves have differing views on it. Some say the whole Qur'ān is structured according to divine inspiration, others say that the specific arrangement of the *sūrahs* was the personal opinion of some of the Prophet's companions—and this idea has been proposed already centuries ago.[156]

It is very interesting that recent scholarship, including Mustansir Mir's *Coherence in the Qur'ān*,[157] Neal Robinson's *Discovering the Qur'ān*,[158] Angelika Neuwirth's encyclopedia entry "Form and Structure,"[159] Michel Cuyper's *The Banquet*,[160] Carl W. Ernst's *How to Read the Qur'ān*[161] and Raymond Farrin's *Structure and Qur'ānic Interpretation*,[162] is revealing a profound structure and coherence within the text possibly unknown to the classical tradition. Taking this most recent book by Farrin as emblematic of this larger body of scholarship, we note that he has summarized the character of the Qur'ānic structure as follows:

> As will become progressively evident, the whole Qur'ān is arranged according to the law of symmetry. Michel Cuypers, drawing on the analysis by Roland Meynet of Biblical texts, has shown that symmetry manifests itself in the Qur'ān in three ways:
>
> 1) according to parallelism, whereby the structure takes the form AB/A'B'
>
> 2) by chiasmus, or inverted parallelism whereby the structure takes the form AB/B'A'

3) by concentrism, which is like chiasmus but includes a unique central element: AB/C/B′A′[163]

Bringing such analysis to bear on the entirety of the Qur'ānic text, Farrin has remarked:

> Again, symmetry is the rule; it obtains in chapters and pairs, just as it obtains in groups, systems, and the Book as a whole. Considering the total pattern of these relationships, we may speak of a dense interconnection within a single comprehensive design. The Qur'ān's structure, it becomes apparent, is at once characterized by great complexity and pure simplicity.[164]

In his conclusion, having identified a general concentrism structuring the text as a whole, Farrin has further remarked:

> We see that the Qur'ān is a text whose form perfectly supports its meaning. The five main points, as we have noticed, all point to God: The beginning calls on Him, the ending seeks refuge in Him, the middles of the two systems are oriented to the place of His manifestation on earth, and the center is oriented to Him above. Correspondences are numerous and dense, to be sure, but overall they follow a single concentric plan. Parallels and symmetries throughout underscore a greater unity. Every formal element refers to the One God.[165]

In agreement with the stylometric studies previously referenced, Farrin has, on the basis of textual structure and unity, similarly judged:

> We have seen that a structural logic of symmetry is seen on the level of the chapter, pair, group, system, and the text as a whole. This consistency in underlying structure strongly suggests that the text did not have multiple authors. In short, our study offers further evidence that the entire Qur'ān, form and content, traces directly to the Prophet.[166]

Let us give the final word on this topic to Michel Cuypers,

who perhaps more than anyone has furthered this type of rhetorical analysis into the structure of the Qur'ān:

> The Islamic tradition speaks of the 'inimitability' (*i'jāz*) of the Qur'an. This is, above all, a dogma expressing faith in the divine origin of the text that, by this fact alone, can only be unique, without an equivalent. We have not used nor discussed this expression in this book, which is strictly literary. It is true, however, that through assiduous reading and textual analysis the exceptionally complex and erudite character of this text has become more and more evident to us. We can no longer endorse what Voltaire wrote in his *Dictionnaire philosophique*: "The Qur'an is a rhapsody without connections, without order, without art." We hope to have demonstrated that, in spite of the impression that a superficial reading might leave, the Qur'an is a text whose parts *are linked* according to clearly definable principles of *order* and a consummate work of *art* even though it is outside of our Western and modern mental habits.[167]

As a final note, if the deep structure of the Qur'ān analyzed by Farrin, Cuypers and these other scholars is correct, then this, judged in conjunction with the piecemeal reception and arrangement of individual segments of the text, in many cases suited to particular occasions and broadly separated in time, grants evidence to the Qur'ān as a complete, prefigured book apart from its occasions of revelation.

4. B. 3 Question of Scriptural Borrowing

A frequent polemical assumption regarding the Qur'ān, in light of it being historically subsequent to the Jewish and Christian scriptures, is its being simply a derived hodgepodge of the former, lacking revelatory originality. A major difficulty with such a view is that it conflates correlation with causation, as Hamza Mustafa Njozi has noted:

> Similarity between any two compositions or books does not

in itself constitute sufficient evidence that one was copied from the other, or the latter from the earlier one. Both of them could be based on a common third source. And this is precisely the argument of the Qur'ān. There are certain portions of the Bible that might have remained intact and if God is the source of both revelations that should explain the existence of parallels.[168]

Indeed, the entire notion of attribution rests on an underlying, often unspoken assumption of the priority or normativity of one scripture or set of scriptures over another. If the Qur'ān adapts a Biblical story for its own purposes, this might well be viewed as appropriation, but the judgment as to its legitimacy or illegitimacy rests upon the prior question of the Qur'ān's revelatory status—God, after all, can hardly plagiarize from Himself. The entire matter of such judgment may be readily turned on its head, as S. Parvez Manzoor has argued:

> The Arabian outsider "appropriates" the truth of the Bible and "forges" it into a revelation of his own! Everything Qur'ānic that corroborates earlier scriptures, thus, is viewed as "borrowing" and everything that the Qur'ān modifies of their contents is dismissed as "deviant" and "distortive". Should one, on the other hand, accept—even phenomenologically and not doctrinally—that the "founder" of Islam stands at the end of a long chain of religious personalities, best described as "prophetic" according to the typology of the Near East, then the whole edifice of Biblical Orientalism crumbles to the ground. In the latter case, it would be absurd to speak about "derivations", "borrowings", "distortions", even "misunderstandings", as the Qur'ānic revelation too would be recognized as expounding the common truth of "monotheism" (according to the Muslim opinion, even arbitrating it) rather than "transgressing" the preserve of Judaeo-Christianity.[169]

Nor does the claim of borrowing resolve the various sharp distinctions that may be drawn between the Qur'ān and earlier scriptural sources. As Muḥammad Muṣṭafā al-Aʿẓamī has somewhat caustically observed:

> So where exactly does this counterfeiting manifest itself? And concerning appropriations from the Old Testament (as alleged by Wansbrough, Nöldeke, and others), why should the Prophet seek to emulate a Scripture portraying Yahweh as a tribal God, affiliated not even with the Samaritans or Edomites but solely with Israel? At the very opening of the Book we find: "In the Name of Allah, Most Gracious, Most Merciful. Praise be to Allah, the Cherisher and Sustainer of the Worlds." A universal invocation to Allah, transcending tribes and races and based only on the precepts of faith. One cannot pluck such a rich mango from the prickly arms of a parched cactus.[170]

Such adaptation from a common pool of extant source material in the broader oral and written culture in the context of the formation of a presumptive new scripture—a new revelatory discourse—may in fact be recognized as the only way forward for such a project, as Norman O. Brown has argued:

> How do you start a new civilization—in the seventh or the twentieth century CE, with all that history weighing like an Alp on the brains of the living? Out of the rubble of the old; there is no other way.... Massignon speaks of the farrago of folklore (*fatras folkloriste*) in the Koran. First you trash or junk the old, as in *Finnegans Wake*, or the Koran; reducing preexistent traditions to rubble. Muslim piety, for whom the Koran is the supra-historical word of God, is troubled by the question of the relation of the Koran to preexistent traditions. Western historicism, with its well-honed methods of source criticism—*Quellenforschung*—is only too delighted to lose itself in tracing the Koran to its sources, with the usual nihilistic result: the Koran is reduced to a meaningless confusion.... The notion that Muhammad was a charlatan, who stole from the treasury of Western Civilization and passed off his

plagiarisms on his unsophisticated Bedouin audience as the voice of God, is still very much alive at the back of Western minds. Muslim piety need not be so troubled, nor Western scholarship so complacent and condescending.[171]

Some Western scholars, at least, are sensitive to the issue at hand. As William A. Graham has noted:

Following closely upon, and closely related to, this concern with the text and language of the Qur'ān has been a particular kind of historical interest that stands out as perhaps the major emphasis of non-Muslim Qur'ān study. This is the inquiry into the "background" or "origin" of the Qur'ān: the study of major ideas and specific details of the Qur'ān in *their relation* to—or, as non-Muslim scholarship has tended to see it, *their derivation from*—older cultural and religious sources, pre-eminently those of the Jewish and Christian traditions. In the massive literature produced with this kind of problem in view, one can discern perhaps most easily of anywhere some of the often quite unconscious cultural and religious biases of non-Muslim Qur'ānic studies as a whole. Specifically, the implication in such work is often that if historical derivation can be shown, the "dependence" of the later tradition(s) of Islam on Christian or Jewish predecessors is thereby proven, thus undermining the distinctive and creative character of the later tradition or even its transcendent dimension (i.e., by showing its temporal "origin").[172]

Similarly, as Fred M. Donner has observed:

I sometimes get the uneasy feeling, as I read recent work on the Qur'ān, that some of it is a little too enthusiastic about finding simplistic textual parallels, without bothering to ask about all the other dimensions of cultural transmission: the omissions, selectivity, transformations, etc. This satisfaction with superficial "borrowings" smacks of the kind of reductionist approach... (now focused more on Christian parallels, rather than the Jewish parallels that were more popular in the early twentieth century), and the unseemly enthusiasm that

is sometimes palpable in such writings suggests that these authors are motivated on some deep, personal level not so much
by the historian's desire to understand Islam and the Qur'ān,
as by the polemicist's desire to diminish, discredit, or refute
Islam.[173]

4. B. 4 Receptiveness of the Reader

A given reader will, in the nature of things, bring to his
encounter with the Qur'ān his own presuppositions, biases
and general receptiveness in a way that may immediately
and decisively color his experience of the text, in severe
cases blocking it entirely. In this regard, speaking of the
hermeneutical challenge of understanding the Qur'ān and its
meaning, Henri Corbin has critically observed that "the mode
of understanding [of the Qur'ān] is conditioned by the mode
of being of him who understands."[174]

The same observation was made long before by Jalāl al-Dīn
Rūmī as well:

> The Qur'ān is like a bride. Although you pull the veil away
> from her face, she does not show herself to you. When
> you investigate the Qur'ān, but receive no joy or mystical
> unveiling, it is because your pulling at the veil has caused you
> to be rejected. The Qur'ān has deceived you and shown itself
> as ugly. It says, "I am not a beautiful bride." It is able to show
> itself in any form it desires. But if you stop pulling at its veil
> and seek its good pleasure; if you water its field, serve it from
> afar and strive in that which pleases it, then it will show you
> its face without any need for you to draw aside its veil.[175]

Much the same reflection was offered even earlier by Abū
Naṣr al-Sarrāj:

> The people of understanding among the people of knowledge
> know that the only way to correctly connect to that to
> which the Qur'ān guides us is by pondering, reflecting, being
> wakeful, recollecting and being present with the heart when

reciting the Qur'ān. They know this as well from His words, *A book which We have sent down to you as a blessing so that they might ponder its verses and so that those who possess understanding might recollect* [38:29]. Pondering, reflecting and recollecting are only possible through the heart being present because God said, *surely in that there is a remembrance for one who has a heart or will lend an ear with presence* [50:37], that is to say, one who is present with the heart.[176]

Commenting upon the receptivity to the meaning of the Book present in a true spiritual hermeneutics, Patrick Laude has noted:

> Spiritual hermeneutics is a reciprocal and gradual actualization of the unfathomable depth of scriptural meaning and the spiritual consciousness of the reader. More specifically, a meditative contact with the Qur'ān discloses her own true nature to the soul, by actualizing her relationship with her Lord, that is the aspect of the Divine that "faces" the soul and constitutes her deepest ontological and spiritual ground. In reverse, the believer, through *lectio divina*, actualizes layers and aspects of the sacred text that lie within its inexhaustible wealth of meaning. Reading Scripture means to reconduct inward what is outward, i.e., to operate a kind of inner "reconversion" of the linguistic form of the Scripture. Such an inward reversion is precisely possible because the letter of the Qur'ān is none other than the analytic and external manifestation of the *haqīqah*, the true meaning of the text.[177]

In a more general way, Christopher Buck has commented upon the dynamic of approaching the Qur'ān:

> An understanding of the Qur'ān is analogous to music appreciation, although saying so is by no means meant to trivialize the purpose or process of gaining that understanding. Muslims have a coherent worldview, one that originates from the Qur'ān itself. To appreciate the Qur'ān is to develop a sensitivity to the operation of the divine in a culture removed for centuries from the Euro-American world but now increas-

ingly an integral part of it. One can only gain from such an understanding. Indeed, one can only be enriched by it, but only if one's prejudices are first abandoned. The Qur'ān is a world unto itself, a palatial architecture of meaning that is multidimensional and comprehends the totality of the human experience. On the moral and spiritual foundation of the Qur'ān, an entire history and civilization has been built. The West can continue to clash with Islam—which is the religion of the Qur'ān—or embrace it. To acknowledge the beauty and depth of the Qur'ān is not to convert to Islam, but to converse with it and with Muslims who are enlivened by it.[178]

SURAH YUNUS, 10: 9–10

5

Conclusion

Let us review the ground covered. In considering the Qur'ān in light of secularity, we have argued that such a worldview—however taken for granted in the contemporary context—suffers from multiple philosophical failings that may be judged to be collectively fatal to its very coherence. These include its unwarranted and often unreflective pre-commitment to immanent closure, the incompleteness and incoherence—particularly in the foundational domains of consciousness, reason and meaning—inherent in its secular commitments, and its inability to accommodate key traces or pointers to transcendence. In a more specific context, re-lated to that of the secular historian, there are a number of problematic issues that may additionally be addressed. These include the tendency of empiricism toward an implicit anti-supernaturalism, the incoherence of claims to scholarly objectivity in light of the very embeddedness of such schol-arship in its own cultural and historical particularity, the tenuousness of much of what passes for secular historical judgment, and the failure of recognition of the Qur'ān's own judgment upon the secular historian who has rejected the transcendent.

In considering the Qur'ān in light of its own context, we have reviewed a number of societal considerations that may serve as so many pointers with regard to its revelatory status. Following an initial presentation of arguments for the reliable codification and preservation of the Qur'ānic text, we have noted its lack of cultural precedent, the decisiveness of its impact in fundamentally altering the character of Arab society, its fecundity across multiple Islamic civilizations in the generation of virtue and sanctity, and its similar fecundity in the generation of formal beauty as reflected in architecture, the arts and even the commonplace details of daily life. We have further reviewed a number of doctrinal considerations that may similarly serve as pointers with regard to the Qur'ān's revelatory status. These include the inherent metaphysical evidence of its core doctrinal claim of Divine Unity, the universality of its religious vision across multiple traditions, the completeness of its discourse in relation to the religious life, the coordination of its expression regarding the Divine nature and attributes with that found in classical philosophical theism, and the possible tentative correlation of certain of its physical descriptions with the findings of modern science.

In considering the Qur'ān in light of the Messenger, we have reviewed a number of points of distinctiveness between the two. These include the evident distinctiveness of voice between the Qur'ān and the most reliably recorded statements of Muhammad, a distinctiveness that has been formally confirmed through statistical stylometric analysis and further reflected in the evident distinction of personality between the Qur'ān and Muhammad. Additionally, the rare instances of past and future knowledge communicated by the Qur'ān stand in sharp distinction to the possible knowledge of Muhammad. The position of Muhammad, in terms of his consistently reported character, the effect of proclaiming the Qur'ānic message against his own best interests, his own unletteredness, lack of learning and lack of poetic gifts and, further, the extreme implausibility of his receiving external instruction, all speak against the possibility of his own authorship.

In considering the Qur'ān in light of its auditors and

readers, we have reviewed a number of positive judgments that may be made upon the Qur'ān. These include the recognized unparalleled excellence of its Arabic expression, the near-exhaustive richness of its use of the possibilities of the Arabic language, the interpenetrative and simultaneous character of the core Qur'ānic message as it appears throughout the text, its own extensive use of argument and rhetorical strategies of persuasion, and the felt experience of presence that it frequently evokes. We have further reviewed a number of negative judgments upon the Qur'ān and responses that may be given to these, including the problematic issue of its expressive quality in translation, the challenge of its apparent textual incoherence, the assertion of scriptural borrowing and the matter of a reader's receptiveness to the text.

Few of these considerations rise to the level of philosophic proof, but at best might be taken as highly persuasive. Further, the considerations are of varying strengths of appeal and of varying degrees of directness in addressing the nature of the Qur'ān. Means of escaping the conclusions to which they point may in certain instances be found. The whole is an exercise in laying out a persuasive case, so far as it may be accomplished. The act of judgment, of weighing the case presented in its entirety, belongs necessarily to the reader. These considerations, presented—if in summary—in their comprehensive entirety, may well be judged as providing a sufficiently persuasive case supporting the claim of the Qur'ān as truly revealed. What further conclusions the reader may existentially draw from this are a matter of personal judgment as well as conscience.

References

1. Arthur O. Lovejoy, *The Great Chain of Being: The Study of the History of an Idea* (Cambridge, MA: Harvard University Press, 1933), p. 7; also James W. Sire, *Naming the Elephant: Worldview as a Concept* (Downers Grove, IL: InterVarsity Press, 2004).

2. Charles Taylor, *A Secular Age* (Cambridge, MA: Harvard University Press, 2007), p. 25.

3. Ibid., p. 590.

4. Ibid., p. 549.

5. Edward Feser, *Scholastic Metaphysics: A Contemporary Introduction* (Neunkirchen-Seelscheid, Germany: Editiones Scholasticae, 2014), p. 23.

6. C. Stephen Evans, *The Historical Christ and the Jesus of Faith: The Incarnational Narrative as History* (Oxford, UK: Oxford University Press, 1996), p. 187, n. 241.

7. Ibid., n. 243.

8. For further analysis, see C. Stephen Evans, *The Historical Christ and the Jesus of Faith*, ch. 8 ("Critical History and the Supernatural"); also Alvin Plantinga, *Warranted Christian Belief* (Oxford, UK: Oxford University Press, 2000), ch. 12 ("Two (or More) Kinds of Scripture Scholarship").

9. William A. Graham, "Those Who Study and Teach the Qur'ān," in his *Islamic and Comparative Religious Studies: Selected Writings* (Farnham, UK: Ashgate, 2010), p. 8 (http://dash.harvard.edu/bitstream/handle/1/4483169/Graham_ThoseWhoStudyQuran.pdf).

10. See J. P. Moreland, "The Image of God and the Failure of Scientific Atheism," in William Lane Craig and Chad Meister (eds.), *God is Great; God is Good: Why Belief in God is Reasonable and Responsible* (Downers Grove, IL: InterVarsity Press, 2009), pp. 32–41.

11. John Searle, *Freedom and Neurobiology* (New York: Columbia University Press, 2007), pp. 4–5.

12. J. P. Moreland, *The Recalcitrant Imago Dei: Human Persons and the Failure of Naturalism*, (London: SCM Press, 2009), p. 20.

13. J. P. Moreland, "A Reluctant Traveler's Guide for Slouching Towards Theism: A Philosophical Note on Nagel's *Mind and Cosmos*," *Philosophia Christi* 14 (2): 435–6 (2012); see also Thomas Nagel, *Mind and Cosmos: Why the Materialist Neo-Darwinian Conception of Nature is Almost Certainly False* (Oxford, UK: Oxford University Press, 2012), ch. 4 ("Cognition").

14. Victor Reppert, "The Argument from Reason," in William Lane Craig and J. P. Moreland (eds.), *The Blackwell Companion to Natural Theology*, (Malden, MA: Blackwell, 2009), pp. 344–90; Victor Reppert, *C. S. Lewis's Dangerous Idea: In Defense of the Argument from Reason* (Downers Grove, IL: InterVarsity Press, 2003); Alvin Plantinga, *Where the Conflict Really Lies:*

Science, Religion, and Naturalism (Oxford, UK: Oxford University Press, 2011).

15. See Angus Menuge, "Libertarian Free Will and the Argument from Reason" (http://tinyurl.com/menuge-libertarian); Angus Menuge, "Reason Cannot Be Located In a Materialist World" (http://tinyurl.com/menuge-located); Angus Menuge, "The Ontological Argument from Reason: Why Compatibilist Accounts of Reasoning Fail," *Philosophia Christi* 13 (1): 59–74 (2011); J. P. Moreland, *The Recalcitrant Imago Dei*, ch. 4.

16. See James Ross, "The Immaterial Aspects of Thought," *The Journal of Philosophy* 89 (3): 136–50 (1992); Edward Feser, "Kripke, Ross, and the Immaterial Aspects of Thought," *American Catholic Philosophical Quarterly* 87 (1): 1–32 (2013).

17. James W. Sire, *The Universe Next Door: A Basic Worldview Catalog*, 5th Ed. (Downers Grove, IL: InterVarsity Press, 2009), pp. 111–3.

18. John F. Haught, *Is Nature Enough?: Meaning and Truth in the Age of Science* (Cambridge, UK: Cambridge University Press, 2006), pp. 194–5.

19. John F. Haught, *God and the New Atheism: A Critical Response to Dawkins, Harris, and Hitchens* (Louisville, KY: Westminster John Knox Press, 2007), p. 23.

20. Roger Scruton, *An Intelligent Person's Guide to Modern Culture* (South Bend, IN: St. Augustine's Press, 1998), p. 68.

21. Graham Dunstan Martin, *Living on Purpose: Meaning, Intention, Value* (Edinburgh, UK: Floris Books, 2008), p. 47.

22. Stephen Jay Gould, *Rocks of Ages: Science and Religion in the Fullness of Life* (New York: Ballantine Books, 2002), p. 5.

23. Kenneth L. Woodward, *The Book of Miracles: The Meaning of the Miracle Stories in Christianity, Judaism, Buddhism, Hinduism and Islam* (New York: Simon & Schuster, 2001).

24. Craig S. Keener, *Miracles: The Credibility of the New Testament Accounts*, 2 vols. (Grand Rapids, MI: Baker Academic, 2011).

25. Ibid., p. 134.

26. Vincent J. Cornell, *Realm of the Saint: Power and Authority in Moroccan Sufism* (Austin: University Texas Press, 1998).

27. Geoffrey Parrinder, *Mysticism in the World's Religions* (Oxford, UK: Oneworld, 1995).

28. Steven T. Katz (ed.), *Comparative Mysticism: An Anthology of Original Sources* (Oxford, UK: Oxford University Press, 2013).

29. Robert K. C. Forman (ed.), *The Problem of Pure Consciousness: Mysticism and Philosophy* (Oxford, UK: Oxford University Press, 1990); Robert K. C. Forman (ed.), *Mysticism, Mind, Consciousness* (Albany, NY: State University of New York Press, 1997); Robert K. C. Forman (ed.), *The Innate Capacity: Mysticism, Philosophy and Psychology* (Oxford, UK: Oxford University Press, 1998).

30. www.peterkreeft.com/topics-more/20_arguments-gods-existence.htm.

31. http://tinyurl.com/plantinga24.

32. Edward Feser, *Aquinas: A Beginner's Guide* (Oxford, UK: Oneworld, 2009), ch. 3, "Natural Theology"; see also Edward Feser, *The Last Superstition, A Refutation of the New Atheism* (South Bend, IN: St. Augustine's Press, 2008), ch. 3, "Getting Medieval".

33. Robert J. Spitzer, *New Proofs for the Existence of God: Contributions of Contemporary Physics and Philosophy* (Cambridge, UK: Eerdmans, 2010).

34. Craig S. Keener, *Miracles*, p. 102.

35. C. Stephen Evans, *The Historical Christ and the Jesus of Faith*, p. 177.

36. David Bentley Hart, *Atheist Delusions: The Christian Revolution and Its Fashionable Enemies* (New Haven, CT: Yale University Press, 2010), p. 102.

37. Peter Berger, "Some Second Thoughts on Substantive versus Functional Definitions of Religion," *Journal for the Scientific Study of Religion* 13 (2): 125–33 (1974), p. 129.

38. Edward Said, *Covering Islam: How the Media and the Experts Determine How We See the Rest of the World* (New York: Vintage Books, 1997), pp. 23–4; see also Muḥammad Muṣṭafā al-Aʿẓamī, *The History of the Qurʾānic Text*, ch. 19; also Muḥammad Mohar Ali, *The Qurʾān and the Orientalists: An Examination of their Main Theories and Assumptions* (Ipswich, UK: Jamʾiat 'Iḥyaaʾ Minhaaj al-Sunnah, 2004); also Abdul Latif Tibawi, *English-Speaking Orientalists: A Critique of Their Approach to Islam and Arab Nationalism* (Geneva: Islamic Centre, 1965).

39. Leo Strauss, *Natural Right and History* (Chicago, IL: University of Chicago Press, 1953), p. 25.

40. Jon D. Levenson, "The Bible: Unexamined Commitments of Criticism," *First Things* 30: 24–33, Feb. 1993 (www.firstthings.com/article/1993/02/003-the-bible-unexamined-commitments-of-criticism).

41. Peter L. Berger, *A Rumor of Angels: Modern Society and the Rediscovery of the Supernatural* (New York: Doubleday, 1969), p. 51.

42. Ibid., pp. 52–3.

43. Jon D. Levenson, *The Hebrew Bible, the Old Testament, and Historical Criticism: Jews and Christians in Biblical Studies* (Louisville, KY: Westminster John Knox Press, 1993), pp. 116–7.

44. William A. Graham, "Those Who Study and Teach the Qurʾān," p. 6.

45. Peter Van Inwagen, "Skeptical of the Skeptics" (review of *The Historical Christ and the Jesus of Faith: The Incarnational Narrative as History* by C. Stephen Evans), *Books & Culture* 3: 29–30, May 1997 (http://andrewm bailey.com/pvi/Skeptical.pdf).

46. Muzaffar Iqbal, "The Qurʾān, Orientalism, and the Encyclopaedia of the Qurʾān," *Journal of Qurʾānic Research and Studies* 3 (5): 5–45 (2008) (www.cis-ca.org/muzaffar/EQ-Rev.pdf).

47. Walid A. Saleh, "The Etymological Fallacy and Qur'ānic Studies: Muhammad, Paradise, and Late Antiquity," in Angelika Neuwirth, et al. (eds.), *The Qur'ān in Context: Historical and Literary Investigations into the Qur'ānic Milieu* (Leiden: Brill, 2010), pp. 649–98 (https://utoronto.academia.edu/WalidSaleh).
48. Walid A. Saleh, "A Piecemeal Qur'ān: Furqan and Its Meaning in Classical Islam and Modern Qur'ānic Studies," *Jerusalem Studies in Arabic and Islam* 42: 31–71 (2015) (https://utoronto.academia.edu/WalidSaleh).
49. Mircea Eliade, *The Quest: History and Meaning in Religion* (Chicago, IL: University of Chicago Press, 1969), p. 62.
50. Muzaffar Iqbal, "The Qur'ān, Orientalism, and the Encyclopaedia of the Qur'ān," pp. 21–2; see also Muzaffar Iqbal, "The Qur'ān and Its Disbelievers," *Islam & Science* 7 (2): 123–4 (2009) (http://tinyurl.com/iqbal-disbel).
51. Jonathan A. C. Brown, *Hadith: Muhammad's Legacy in the Medieval and Modern World* (Oxford, UK: Oneworld, 2009), p. 197.
52. Muḥammad Muṣṭafā al-Aʿẓamī, *The History of the Qur'ānic Text*, p. 341.
53. Muzaffar Iqbal, "Western Academia and the Qur'ān: Some Enduring Prejudices," *The Muslim World Book Review* 30 (1): 10 (2009) (www.cisca.org/muzaffar/eq2.pdf).
54. Ibid.
55. William C. Chittick, "The Koran as the Lover's Mirror," in Patrick Laude (ed.), *Universal Dimensions of Islam: Studies in Comparative Religion* (Bloomington, IN: World Wisdom, 2011), p. 67.
56. Mark Anderson, *Pure: Modernity, Philosophy and the One* (San Rafael, CA: Sophia Perennis, 2009), p. 71; see ibid., ch. 10 ("Purification"), pp. 71–106; see also Pierre Hadot, *Philosophy as a Way of Life: Spiritual Exercises from Socrates to Foucault* (Malden, MA: Blackwell, 1995); also Pierre Hadot, *The Present Alone is Our Happiness*, 2nd Ed. (Stanford, CA: Stanford University Press, 2011).
57. Ibid., p. 74.
58. Alan Jones, "The Qur'ān-II," in A. F. L. Beeston, et al. (eds.), *Cambridge History of Arabic Literature: Arabic Literature to the End of the Umayyad Period* (Cambridge, UK: Cambridge University Press, 2010), pp. 240–41.
59. See Liaquat Ali Khan, "*Hagarism*: The Story of a Book Written by Infidels for Infidels," (on Patricia Crone) *The Daily Star* 5 (680), April 28, 2006 (http://tinyurl.com/khan-hagarism); also Patricia Crone, "What do we actually know about Mohammed?" (www.opendemocracy.net/faith-europe_islam/mohammed_3866.jsp).
60. Robert G. Hoyland, *Seeing Islam as Others Saw It: A Survey and Evaluation of Christian, Jewish and Zoroastrian Writings on Early Islam* (Princeton, NJ: The Darwin Press, 1997), p. 591.

61. B. Sadeghi & U. Bergmann, "The Codex of a Companion of the Prophet and the Qur'ān of the Prophet," *Arabica* 57 (4): 343–436 (2010); B. Sadeghi & M. Goudarzi, "Ṣan'ā' 1 and the Origins of the Qur'ān," *Der Islam* 87 (1–2): 1–129 (2012).

62. http://tinyurl.com/tuebingen-koran *and* http://tinyurl.com/birmingham-quran.

63. F. E. Peters, "The Quest of the Historical Muhammad," *International Journal of Middle East Studies* 23 (3): 298–9 (1991).

64. François De Blois, "Islam in Its Arabian context," in Angelica Neuwirth, et al. (eds.), *The Qur'ān in Context: Historical and Literary Investigations into the Qur'ānic Milieu* (Leiden: Brill, 2010), p. 618.

65. From William Muir, *Life of Mahomet,* cited in M. A. Draz, *Introduction to the Qur'ān* (London: I. B. Tauris, 2011), pp. 17–8.

66. Kenneth Cragg, *The Mind of the Qur'ān,* (London: George Allen & Unwin, 1973), p. 26.

67. See Muḥammad Muṣṭafā al-A'ẓamī, *The History of the Qur'ānic Text*, p. 192; see also Ingrid Mattson, *The Story of the Qur'ān: Its History and Place in Muslim Life*, 2nd Ed. (Hoboken, NJ: Wiley-Blackwell, 2013), pp. 79–85.

68. Adrian Brockett, "Value of Ḥafṣ and Warsh Transmissions," in Andrew Rippin (ed.), *Approaches to the History of the Interpretation of the Qur'ān* (Oxford, UK: Clarendon Press, 1988), p. 44.

69. Cited in Muḥammad Muṣṭafā al-A'ẓamī, *The History of the Qur'ānic Text*, p. 12.

70. John Wansbrough, *Qur'ānic Studies: Sources and Methods of Scriptural Interpretation* (Amherst, NY: Prometheus Books, 2004), p. 203.

71. François De Blois, "Islam in Its Arabian context," in Angelica Neuwirth, et al. (eds.), *The Qur'ān in Context: Historical and Literary Investigations into the Qur'ānic Milieu* (Leiden: Brill, 2010), p. 618.

72. Angelika Neuwirth, "Structural, Linguistic and Literary Features" in Jane Dammen McAuliffe (ed.), *The Cambridge Companion to the Qur'ān* (Cambridge, Cambridge University Press, 2006), p. 100.

73. M. A. S. Abdel Haleem, interview (www.halalmonk.com/mas-abdel-haleem-the-language-of-the-quran).

74. Angelika Neuwirth, personal interview, cited in http://tinyurl.com/tzortzis-testimony.

75. F. E. Peters, *Muhammad and the Origins of Islam* (Albany, NY: State University of New York Press, 1994), p. 259.

76. Hans Küng, "Muhammad: A Prophet?," in Alan Race and Paul M. Hedges (eds.), *Christian Approaches to Other Faiths* (London: SCM Press, 2008), p. 135.

77. W. Montgomery Watt, *Muhammad at Mecca* (Oxford, UK: Clarendon Press, 1953), p. 80.

78. Frithjof Schuon, *Christianity/Islam: Perspectives on Esoteric Ecumenism* (Bloomington, IN: World Wisdom, 2008), p. 111.
79. Muḥyī al-Dīn ibn al-'Arabī, *Sufis of Andalusia*, tr. R. W. J. Austin (Sherborne, UK: Beshara Publications, 1988).
80. Farīd al-Dīn 'Aṭṭār, *Muslim Saints and Mystics*, tr. A. J. Arberry (London: Arkana, 1990).
81. Michael Sugich, *Signs on the Horizons: Meetings with Men of Knowledge and Illumination* (self-published, 2013).
82. Martin Lings, "Proofs of Islam," *Ilm Magazine* 10 (1): 4 (1985) (http://simerg.com/literary-readings/proofs-of-islam/).
83. W. Montgomery Watt, *Muhammad's Mecca* (Edinburgh, UK: Edinburgh University Press, 1988), p. 1.
84. Martin Lings, "Proofs of Islam," p. 5.
85. Titus Burckhardt, *Sacred Art in East and West* (Louisville, KY: Fons Vitae, 2001), pp. 14–15.
86. A general consideration apart from the Islamic tradition specifically may be found in C. Stephen Evans, *The Historical Christ and the Jesus of Faith*, ch. 9.
87. William C. Chittick, "The Recovery of Human Nature," *Transdisciplinarity in Science and Religion* 4: 285 (2008) (www.academia.edu/7347773/The_Recovery_of_Human_Nature); see also William C. Chittick, *Science of the Cosmos, Science of the Soul* (Oxford, UK: Oneworld, 2007), pp. 111–12.
88. Mircea Eliade, *The Two and the One* (Chicago, IL: University of Chicago Press, 1962), p. 192.
89. Frederick Copleston, *Religion and the One: Philosophies East and West* (New York: Crossroad Publishing, 1982), p. 18.
90. Nasr Abu Zayd, "The Qur'ān, God and Man in Communication: Inaugural Lecture for the Cleveringa Chair at Leiden University (November 27, 2000)," p. 4 (www.let.leidenuniv.nl/forum/01_1/onderzoek/2.htm).
91. See Reza Shah-Kazemi, *The Other in Light of the One: The Universality of the Qur'ān and Interfaith Dialogue* (Cambridge, UK: Islamic Texts Society, 2006).
92. Ernest McClain, *Meditations Through the Qur'ān: Tonal Images in an Oral Culture* (New York: Red Wheel Weiser, 1981), p. 26.
93. T. J. Winter, *Al-Ghazali: Remembrance of Death and the Afterlife* (Rumi Productions Lecture Set (2003), disc 3, track 4).
94. T. J. Winter, *Al-Ghazali: Remembrance of Death and the Afterlife* (Rumi Productions Lecture Set (2003), disc 3, track 2).
95. See Brian Leftow, "God, concepts of," in *Routledge Encyclopedia of Philosophy* (http://tinyurl.com/leftow-theism); also Brian Morley, "Western Concepts of God," in *Internet Encyclopedia of Philosophy* (www.iep.utm.edu/god-west/).
96. http://edwardfeser.blogspot.com/2010/09/classical-theism.html.

97. David Conway, *The Rediscovery of Wisdom: From Here to Antiquity in Quest of Sophia* (New York: Palgrave, 2000), p. 3.

98. See René Guénon, *Man and His Becoming According to the Vedanta* (Hillsdale, NY: Sophia Perennis, 2004), esp. ch. 24; also John Levy, *The Nature of Man According to the Vedanta* (London: Kegan Paul International, 2004).

99. See Peter Samsel, *A Treasury of Sufi Wisdom: The Path of Unity* (Bloomington, IN: World Wisdom, 2015).

100. Maurice Bucaille, *The Bible, The Qur'ān and Science: The Holy Scriptures Examined in the Light of Modern Knowledge*, 7th Rev. Exp. Ed. (Flushing, NY: Tahrike Tarsile Qur'ān, 2003).

101. cf. Ziauddin Sardar: "Bucaille's assertions are not wild; he is quite objective about his undertaking and remains more or less within the boundaries of common sense," cited in Ziauddin Sardar, *Explorations in Islamic Science* (London: Mansell Publishing, 1989), p. 34.

102. See Keith L. Moore, "A Scientist's Interpretation of References to Embryology in the Qur'ān," *The Journal of the Islamic Medical Association* 18: 15–6, Jan–June, 1986 (http://tinyurl.com/moore-embryo).

103. See Hamza Andreas Tzortzis, "Embryology in the Qur'ān: A Scientific-Linguistic Analysis of Chapter 23," v.2.1b, April, 2012 (http://tinyurl.com/tzortzis-embryo).

104. See Hamza Andreas Tzortzis, "Does the Qur'ān Contain Scientific Miracles?" v.0.9.4, August, 2013 (http://tinyurl.com/tzortzis-miracles).

105. Mohammad Khalifa, *The Sublime Qur'ān and Orientalism* (London: Longman, 1989), p. 18.

106. A. J. Arberry, *The Holy Koran: An Introduction with Selections* (London: George Allen & Unwin Ltd., 1953), pp. 31–2.

107. Halim Sayoud, "Author Discrimination between the Holy Qur'ān and Prophet's Statements," *Literary and Linguistic Computing* 27 (4): 427 (2012) (http://llc.oxfordjournals.org/content/27/4/427.full.pdf); see also http://tinyurl.com/sayoud-ytsummary (summary).

108. Ibid., p. 442.

109. Halim Sayoud, "Was the Qur'ān Written by the Prophet Muhammad" (Draft Report, August 2014) (http://tinyurl.com/sayoud-draft); see also http://sayoud.net/Interesting.html (more recent work).

110. B. Sadeghi, "The Chronology of the Qur'ān, A Stylometric Research Program," *Arabica* 58 (3–4): 288 (2011).

111. See Qur'ān 80: 1–2.

112. M. A. Draz, *Introduction to the Qur'ān*, pp. 130–31 and following; also see, Hamza Mustafa Njozi, *The Sources of the Qur'ān: A Critical Review of the Authorship Theories*, 2nd Ed. (Riyadh: International Islamic Publishing, 2005), pp. 59–62.

113. See Qur'ān 24: 11–18.

114. Martin Lings, *Muhammad: His Life Based on the Earliest Sources,* (London: George Allen & Unwin, 1983), pp. 77–8.
115. M. S. M. Saifullah, 'Abdullah David & Elias Karim, "Qur'ānic Accuracy vs. Biblical Error: The Kings & Pharaohs of Egypt" (http://tinyurl.com/quranaccuracy).
116. Toby Mayer, "Review Article: *The Qur'ān and its Interpretative Tradition* by Andrew Rippin," *Journal of Qur'ānic Studies* 4 (2): 98 (2002).
117. Hamza Mustafa Njozi, *The Sources of the Qur'ān*, p. 58.
118. Maurice Bucaille, *The Bible, the Qur'ān and Science*, p. 156.
119. Mohammad Khalifa, *The Sublime Qur'ān and Orientalism*, p. 17.
120. W. Montgomery Watt, *Muhammad at Mecca*, p. 52.
121. Muhammad Muhsin Khan, *Ṣaḥīḥ al-Bukhārī: The Translation of the Meanings of Ṣaḥīḥ al-Bukhārī*, Vol. 8 (Lubnān: Dār al-'Arabīyah, 1985), p. 311.
122. Martin Lings, *Muhammad*, p. 276; see also ibid., pp. 274–9.
123. Hamza Mustafa Njozi, *The Sources of the Qur'ān*, p. 37.
124. Ernest McClain, *Meditations Through the Qur'ān*, p. 19.
125. Navid Kermani "Poetry and Language," in Andrew Rippin (ed.), *The Blackwell Companion to the Qur'ān* (Malden, MA: Blackwell, 2009), p. 108.
126. Muḥammad Taqī 'Usmānī, *An Approach to the Qur'ānic Sciences: Uloom-ul-Qur'ān* (Karachi: Darul Isha'at, 2000), p. 261.
127. M. A. S. Abdel Haleem, interview (www.halalmonk.com/mas-abdel-haleem-the-language-of-the-quran).
128. Jamal Badawi, "The Qur'ān the Ultimate Miracle," sec. 10.8, "Source of the Qur'ān VII—Learning from Others" (http://tinyurl.com/badawi-learning).
129. Ibid.; see also Jamal Badawi, *Muhammad's Prophethood: An Analytical View* (Riyadh: World Assembly of Muslim Youth, 1995), pp. 16–19; also Jeffrey Lang, *Losing My Religion: A Call for Help* (Beltsville, MD: Amana, 2004), pp. 312–14.
130. Martin R. Zammit, *A Comparative Lexical Study of Qur'ānic Arabic* (Leiden: Brill, 2002), p. 37.
131. Jane D. McAuliffe, "Introduction," in Jane D. McAuliffe (ed.), *The Cambridge Companion to the Qur'ān* (Cambridge, UK: Cambridge University Press, 2006), p. 6.
132. Kristina Nelson, *The Art of Reciting the Qur'ān* (Austin, TX: University of Texas Press, 1985), p. 7.
133. See Navid Kermani, "The Aesthetic Perception of the Qur'ān as Reflected in Early Muslim History," in Issa J. Boullata (ed.), *Literary Structures of Religious Meaning in the Qur'ān* (Surrey, UK: Curzon Press, 2000); see also, Navid Kermani, *God is Beautiful: The Aesthetic Experience of the Qur'ān* (Cambridge, UK: Polity Press, 2015).
134. Nasr Abu Zayd, "The Qur'ān, God and Man in Communication," p. 6.
135. Shabbir Akhtar, *The Qur'ān and the Secular Mind*, p. 144.

136. Kasim Randeree, "Oral and Written Traditions in Preservation of Qur'ān," *The International Journal of the Book* 7 (4): 11–2 (2010) (http://tinyurl.com/kr-oralwritten; refer to article for extensive references in quoted section).
137. Abdul Wadod Shalabi, *Islam: Religion of Life* (Chicago, IL: Starlatch Press, 2001), p. 30.
138. Seyyed Hossein Nasr, *Ideals and Realities of Islam* (Wellingborough, UK: Thorsons Publishing, 1994), p. 47.
139. Kristina Nelson, *The Art of Reciting the Qur'ān*, pp. 5–6.
140. Norman O. Brown, "The Apocalypse of Islam," in his *Apocalypse and/or Metamorphosis* (Berkeley, CA: University of California Press, 1991), pp. 88–90.
141. See, for instance, Jacques Jomier, "Argument and Persuasion," in his *The Great Themes of the Qur'ān* (London: SCM Press, 1997); see also M. Shahid Alam, "Pragmatic Arguments in the Qur'ān for Belief", July 26, 2011 (http://ssrn.com/abstract=1895559).
142. Rosalind Ward Gwynne, *Logic, Rhetoric and Legal Reasoning in the Qur'ān* (London: RoutledgeCurzon, 2004).
143. Ibid., pp. ix–x.
144. Ibid., p. xii.
145. Ibid.
146. Ibid., pp. xii–xiii.
147. Ibid., p. 203.
148. Seyyed Hossein Nasr, *Ideals and Realities of Islam*, p. 51.
149. Sh. Abdal Hakim Murad [T. J. Winter], "Ramadan Qur'ān Intensive" (http://tinyurl.com/ahm-intensive, 9:00); see also Hasan Askari, *Alone to Alone*, (Pudsey, UK: Seven Mirrors, 1991), p. 113.
150. Fred M. Denny, "The Spiritual-Intellectual Hospitality of Islam and Muslims: Reflections of a Christian Scholar," *Youngstown papers in Islamic Religion, History, and Culture*, Vol. 1 (Youngstown, OH: Youngstown State University, 2005), pp. 11–12.
151. Michael Sells, *Approaching the Qur'ān: The Early Revelations* (Ashland, OR: White Cloud Press, 1999), p. 2.
152. Karen Armstrong, *A History of God* (New York: Ballantine Books, 1994), p. 144.
153. Michael Sells, *Approaching the Qur'ān*, pp. 2–3.
154. T. J. Winter, "The Theology of the Koran" (www.loveofwisdom.co.uk/uploads/2/9/8/1/2981453/theology.doc).
155. Frithjof Schuon, *Understanding Islam* (Bloomington, IN: World Wisdom, 2003), pp. 40–41.
156. M. A. S. Abdel Haleem, interview (www.halalmonk.com/mas-abdel-haleem-the-language-of-the-quran); see also Sh. Abdal Hakim Murad,

"Ramadan Qur'ān Intensive–2/3" (http://tinyurl.com/ahm-qintensive2, 26:30).

157. Mustansir Mir, *Coherence in the Qur'ān* (Indianapolis, IN: American Trust Publications, 1986).
158. Neal Robinson, *Discovering the Qur'ān: a Contemporary Approach to a Veiled Text*, 2nd Ed. (Washington, DC: Georgetown University Press, 2004).
159. Angelika Neuwirth, "Form and Structure," in Jane D. McAuliffe (ed.), *The Encyclopaedia of the Qur'ān*, Vol. 2 (Leiden, Brill, 2002), pp. 245–66.
160. Michel Cuypers, *The Banquet: A Reading of the Fifth Sura of the Qur'ān* (Miami, FL: Convivium Press, 2009); see also Michel Cuypers, *The Composition of the Qur'an: Rhetorical Analysis* (London: Bloomsbury Academic, 2015).
161. Carl. W. Ernst, *How to Read the Qur'ān: A New Guide, with Select Translations* (Chapel Hill, NC: University of North Carolina Press, 2011).
162. Raymond Farrin, *Structure and Qur'ānic Interpretation: A Study of Symmetry and Coherence in Islam's Holy Text* (Ashland, OR: White Cloud Press, 2014).
163. Ibid., p. xv.
164. Ibid., p. 57.
165. Ibid., p. 70.
166. Ibid., p. 71.
167. Michel Cuypers, *The Composition of the Qur'an*, pp. 181–2; for a general treatment of this type of symmetry in other ancient texts of the Near East, see Mary Douglas, *Thinking in Circles: An Essay on Ring Composition* (New Haven, CT: Yale University Press, 2007).
168. Hamza Mustafa Njozi, *The Sources of the Qur'ān*, p. 74.
169. S. Parvez Manzoor, "Method Against Truth: Orientalism and Qur'ānic Studies," *Muslim World Book Review* 7 (4): 33–49 (1987) (www.pmanzoor.info/Method-Truth.htm).
170. Muḥammad Muṣṭafā al-Aʿẓamī, *The History of the Qur'ānic Text*, p. 308; see also Hamza Mustafa Njozi, *The Sources of the Qur'ān*, ch. 11 ("The Problem of Parallels").
171. Norman O. Brown, "The Apocalypse of Islam," p. 91.
172. William A. Graham, "Those Who Study and Teach the Qur'ān"; see also Walid A. Saleh, "The Etymological Fallacy and Qur'ānic Studies," and Walid A. Saleh, "A Piecemeal Qur'ān".
173. Fred M. Donner, "The Historian, the Believer, and the Qur'ān," in Gabriel Said Reynolds (ed.), *New Perspectives on the Qur'ān* (New York: Routledge, 2011), p. 39.
174. Henri Corbin, *History of Islamic Philosophy* (London: Kegan Paul International, 1993), p. 1.

175. Jalāl ad-Dīn Rūmī, *Fihi Ma Fihi* (tr. T.J. Winter); see also T.J. Winter's further comments at http://tinyurl.com/ahm-qintensive1 (8:00) and http://tinyurl.com/ahm-qintensive2 (55:30).

176. Kristin Sands, *Sufi Commentaries on the Qur'ān in Classical Islam* (New York: Routledge, 2006), pp. 30–31.

177. Patrick Laude, "Reading the Qur'ān: The Lessons of the Ambassadors of Mystical Islam," *Sophia: The International Journal for Philosophy of Religion, Metaphysical Theology and Ethics* 46 (2): 154 (2007).

178. Christopher Buck, "Discovering," in Andrew Rippin (ed.), *The Blackwell Companion to the Qur'ān* (Malden, MA: Blackwell, 2006), p. 47.

Index

www.ingramcontent.com/pod-product-compliance
Lightning Source LLC
Chambersburg PA
CBHW032008040426

42448CB00006B/537